BEYOND THE BOOKS

Your Guide to Transition from Academia to Industry

MARY OBIECHINA IFEAKANDU

Copyright © 2025 by Mary Obiechina Ifeakandu

All rights reserved. No part of this publication may be reproduced, stored or transmitted in any form or by any means, electronic, mechanical, photocopying, recording, scanning, or otherwise without written permission from the publisher. It is illegal to copy this book, post it to a website, or distribute it by any other means without permission.

Disclaimer Notice:

Please note that the information contained within this document is for educational and entertainment purposes only. All efforts have been made to present accurate, up-to-date, reliable, and complete information. No warranties of any kind are declared or implied. Readers acknowledge that the author is not engaged in the rendering of legal, financial, medical or professional advice. The content within this book has been derived from various sources. Please consult a licensed professional before attempting any techniques outlined in this book.

By reading this document, the reader agrees that under no circumstances is the author responsible for any losses, direct or indirect, that are incurred as a result of the use of the information contained within this document, including, but not limited to, errors, omissions, or inaccuracies.

First edition

ISBN (print): 978-1-0696841-0-3
ISBN (digital): 978-1-0696841-1-0

Published by MaryEmpowers

Contents

Foreword	vi
Introduction	1
Why Transition?	2
Challenges You Might Face	3
So, How Do You Build the Bridge?	4
What's Beyond the Bridge?	5
CHAPTER 1: Understanding the Transition—Academia vs....	7
Workplace Realities: Comparing Academia and Industry Environments	8
Performance Metrics in Academia & Industry	13
Success Criterion Examination	13
Insights From People in Real Life	16
Insights from Dr. Katrina Armstrong	16
CHAPTER 2: Setting Yourself up for Versatility While in...	18
Understanding Versatility and Identifying Opportunities for Growth	19
Strategies to Cultivate Versatility in Academia	26
Assessing Your Current Skills	28
Learning Skills To Be Versatile	30
Prepare for Transition	32
Document and Reflect on Experiences	34
Insights From Samuel Ogunsola	39
CHAPTER 3: Creating Your Brand	41

Self-Assessment: Know Yourself	41
Boost Your Online Presence	47
Creating Your Brand	48
Networking and Career Advancement Through Personal Branding	54
Insights From Reuben Saba	55
CHAPTER 4: Networking and Mentorship: Building Your Industry...	58
What is the Power of Networks?	59
How Do You Leverage Alumni Networks and Professional Associations	60
How Do Informational Interviews Help in Gaining Industry Insight?	61
Time to Enhance Your Networking Skills	64
Mentorship and Career Success?	68
Insights From Ifeoma Okwor	68
CHAPTER 5: Job Search Strategies—From Application to...	71
Targeting Right Fit	71
Interview Preparation	73
Post-Interview Success	74
Securing the Job	77
Insights From Rachael Erdmann	81
CHAPTER 6: Leveraging Academic Experience for Industry...	84
Consider This Scenario	84
Identifying Your Skills	85
Reviewing Cover Letters and Resumes	86
CHAPTER 7: Navigating the Corporate World—First 90 Days	95
Beginning the First 90 Days: Setting the Stage	96
So, How Do You Align Your Work Style With the Company?	99

    How to Stand Out in the Corporate World?   100
    Adopting a Result-Driven Mindset to Thrive in Industry   102
    Adapting to a Goal-Oriented World to Master
    KPI Evaluations and Objectives   102
    Insights From Reuben Saba and Ifeoma Okwor   105
CHAPTER 8: Overcoming Challenges: Common
Hurdles and...   106
    Overcoming Imposter Syndrome in Your New Role   106
    Potential Challenges During Transition   108
    Climbing the Ladder: Challenges During Career Progression   112
    Maintaining Motivation and Resilience   113
    Insights From Ifeoma Okwor and Samuel Ogunsola   114
CONCLUSION   116
    Your Action Plan for Success   117
REFERENCES   119
About the Author   120

Foreword

Master's and PhD graduates have skills, drive, and a world of opportunities available to them!

However, they often face challenging transitions from academic training to the workforce. They may find themselves feeling lost in a new workplace culture with an unfamiliar value system and differing expectations.

This guidebook by Mary Ifeakandu pinpoints the pain points in an engaging and informative way. She provides real-world examples and suggests practical solutions to help readers make the leap and thrive in their chosen career.

Read the book thoroughly. Complete the exercises thoughtfully. Self-reflect early and often. Then, go and seize your future!

Samantha Pauls, PhD

Introduction

They say you can't have it all. But what if I tell you it's possible?

I've juggled a lot, from pursuing a Ph.D. program while managing a sales team, teaching an entire class of undergraduate students, and attending customer representative calls with a big smile, sometimes all in the same week. It was overwhelming, yes, but it was also exciting.

My craving to paint more on the small canvas of life drove me to experience this whirlwind of academia and industry simultaneously. The sweet spot I sought was the bridge between cutting-edge research and practical application, where theory meets reality, and knowledge creates real-world impact.

Are you ready to move beyond the academic environment and take on the challenges and opportunities in the professional world? *Beyond the Books* is your guide, equipping you to thrive and transition from a specialized academic to a well-rounded professional.

But before we dive deeper, let's clear up a few terms.

When I use the word ***industry***, I'm not just talking about big companies, corporations, or office jobs. I'm referring to the vast and diverse landscape of opportunities that exist **outside the walls of academia**. This includes careers in private companies, government agencies, nonprofits, international organizations, tech startups, hospitals, consulting firms, and many other sectors.

Throughout this book, I will use terms like "**non-academic sector**," "**corporate world,**" and "**professional world**" or "**professional setting.**" While each might sound a little different, in the context of this book, they all point to the same idea: life and career opportunities beyond academia.

- **Non-academic sector** refers to paths outside of teaching and academic research.
- **Corporate world** can bring to mind suits, office buildings, and boardrooms, but here, it simply means structured, career-focused environments outside of academic institutions.
- **Professional world or professional setting** is an umbrella term that encompasses everything from research labs in biotech firms to public health offices to a startup hub, places where people utilize their skills and expertise to create solutions, manage teams, and drive impact.

So, whether I use 'industry', 'non-academic sector', 'corporate world', or 'professional world', I'm talking about the exciting and dynamic space where your academic journey can evolve into something new and meaningful.

It's time to defy the odds and make it happen for you.

Why Transition?

Earning a degree and possessing knowledge in your field is just one part of the equation. The real test comes when you need to apply that knowledge in a professional setting. Being industry-ready while studying or upon completing your degree is essential.

Imagine a graduate holding a degree with extensive knowledge of their field but not knowing how to implement it in the industry. This situation is common and frustrating. I'm not mocking anyone, but students and academics must start bridging the gap between academia and industry.

"And how do I do that?" you ask.

I will guide you through it all in this book.

However, it's important to remember that the academic period teaches you a great deal and prepares you to excel professionally.

The critical thinking, research skills, and resilience you develop in academia are invaluable assets that will support your success in the industry.

Whether you want to diversify your skill set or are drawn to the innovation of a fast-paced environment, transitioning will be a fulfilling experience that will help you gain professional rewards.

Challenges You Might Face

Although transitioning might seem exciting, it does come with its challenges.

Both academic and industry cultures are significantly different. While academia enables you to conduct rigorous research to seek in-depth knowledge, industry allows you to prioritize practical steps to produce tangible results.

During the transition, you may encounter the following challenges:

- **Adapting to shifting priorities:** In academia, the focus is often on gaining a deep understanding of a subject. Conversely, the industry emphasizes meeting deadlines, achieving efficiency, and delivering outcomes. Adjusting to these different priorities can be challenging, but learning to balance thoroughness with productivity is key.
- **Bridging skill set gaps:** While academia develops critical thinking and theoretical knowledge, industry roles often require specific technical skills and the ability to work effectively in teams. Iden-

tifying and addressing these gaps through additional training or practical experience can ease the transition.
- **Gaining practical experience:** Many industry positions require practical experience, which might be limited during academic studies. Seeking internships, part-time work, or project-based learning opportunities can help build relevant knowledge and skills.
- **Understanding work culture differences:** The autonomous nature of academic work contrasts with the structured hierarchy in most industries, where managers assign tasks and expect results. Familiarizing yourself with this dynamic and learning to thrive within it can help make the transition smoother.
- **Developing soft skills:** Effective communication, collaboration, and time management are crucial in the industry, but are often not emphasized in academic settings. Proactively working on these soft skills can enhance your adaptability and success in a professional environment.

So, How Do You Build the Bridge?

With years of experience in changing roles, being versatile, and managing it all efficiently, along with real-life stories of academics who have successfully transitioned to industry, academics in the process of transitioning, and graduate students working towards transitioning after school, I have successfully decoded the process and created a guide to successfully transitioning.

In this book, we will go through the following key aspects to help you successfully transition from academia to industry:

- Understanding the transition
- Adopting versatility
- Self-assessment

INTRODUCTION

- Networking and mentorship
- Job search strategies.
- Navigating the corporate world
- Overcoming challenges
- Leveraging academic experience in the industry

This guide provides actionable insights to help you make a smooth and effective transition. Learn from the experiences of those who have navigated this path before and understand the key strategies for adapting to new roles and environments.

However, let me set the stage by showing you a bigger picture.

What's Beyond the Bridge?

Let's face it. The journey beyond the bridge is not without its challenges. You might even want to return to academia for short courses or projects, which is fine. We continually learn throughout our lives and adopt new skill sets as needed.

However, remember that this book will provide you with ongoing support and resources throughout your career journey, even after you've successfully transitioned into the industry.

So, are you ready to get started? Let's get into it.

Hold On...

Imagine you're in a work setting, and it's been only one week since you joined the company. However, you have spent a month researching a challenging problem your industry has been experiencing. To your surprise, your manager assigns a relatively simple task with a tight deadline.

What would you do?

I'll leave a space for the answer at the end of this book. Let's get going with our book now!

CHAPTER 1: Understanding the Transition—Academia vs. Industry

Transitioning from academia to the industry is akin to switching gears in a vehicle. With a solid understanding and practical skills, one can easily move from one gear to another.

While the ivory tower is alluring with intellectual freedom and in-depth research, the fire to solve real-world problems flickers within almost every curious and practical person.

This chapter compares academic research with workplace performance metrics, highlighting the distinct differences between these two areas. The aim is to equip you with the understanding and confidence to navigate this transition seamlessly.

So, let's get into the details.

Workplace Realities: Comparing Academia and Industry Environments

Academia and industry are two areas where intellectual graduates can excel by applying their knowledge and skills. However, the condition is that each carries completely different goals, structures, and environments, making the transition somewhat challenging.

Highlighting Fundamental Contrasts

Understanding the fundamental differences between the two fields is essential to making an informed decision. The following are vital contrasts to help you navigate this exciting shift:

Focus and priorities:

- **Academia:** In academia, intellectual freedom and deep exploration are paramount. You have the autonomy to delve into complex questions and conduct thorough research to advance knowledge in your field. The primary goal is to make groundbreaking discoveries and contribute to theoretical advancements.
- **Industry**: On the other hand, the industry is all about applying knowledge to create real-world solutions. Collaboration is the norm, with a focus on innovation and practical applications. Your work directly impacts the solution of tangible problems, making your contributions immediately relevant and rewarding.

Structure and decision-making

- **Academia:** Academia operates hierarchically but fosters collaborative decision-making within research groups and departments.

Professors set research agendas, providing a structured yet flexible environment for intellectual exploration and growth.
- **Industry:** The Industry's structure is also hierarchical, although its lines of command and reporting are well-defined. Leaders within the organization often make decisions, but teamwork and collaboration are highly valued as essential to achieving shared goals. This dynamic environment encourages collective effort and innovation.

Work style and pace

- **Academia:** The work style in academia is flexible, and its pace allows for long-term vision and detailed research. This environment nurtures creativity and thorough investigation, providing ample time for developing new ideas and insights.
- **Industry:** Conversely, the industry thrives on a fast-paced, results-driven approach. Projects come with deadlines and milestones that drive efficiency and productivity. Success is measured by the tangible impact of your work, offering a sense of immediate accomplishment and purpose.

Metrics and success criteria

- **Academia**: Here, success is celebrated through publications in prestigious journals, securing grants, making groundbreaking discoveries and receiving citations for your work. These achievements reflect your contribution to the academic community and the advancement of knowledge.
- **Industry**: Success in the sector is measured by real-time outcomes, including revenue growth, market share expansion, and the achievement of key performance indicators (KPIs). Your efforts directly

contribute to the company's success, making your work impactful and fulfilling.

Hear Out Lana...

Meet Lana, a brilliant academic who recently completed her PhD in Biomedical Engineering. Her story of transitioning to the tech industry is both inspiring and enlightening.

"Hello there! During my PhD program, I thrived in the academic environment. I have published research papers, developed innovative methodologies, and gained a deep understanding of my field. The intellectual freedom and lack of pressing deadlines allowed me to explore new ideas and contribute significantly. However, my life took an exciting turn when I joined a tech startup.

The focus shifted from theoretical research to practical applications, and I worked on real-world solutions. The challenges were stimulating, and I quickly adapted to the fast-paced environment.

There were numerous meetings and discussions to ensure the product met the needs of users and industry demands. Of course, the dread of meeting deadlines was always there.

Success in the industry meant having an excellent feature to meet users' needs, even if we had to iterate on the previous plan we had previously rejected.

For instance, I was excited one day because I had finally developed the complex algorithm I had been working on for days. I showed it to the manager, who politely cut me off, saying, "That's nice, but could you please go with a simpler solution?"

A jarring but valuable lesson learned—while academia is about discovering new knowledge, the industry is about delivering results and making a tangible impact.

Do you get the picture?"

Highlighting Work Environment Differences

The work environment differences in both areas are significant. Let's explore them in detail.

Freedom vs. accountability

- **Academia:** Academia offers the freedom to choose your research topics and pursue personal goals. You can freely delve deeply into your studies, contributing new knowledge and advancements in your field. However, accountability is also attainable in academia, depending on the level, such as between Principal Investigators (PIs) and funders, advisors and students, PIs and trainees, and so on.
- **Industry: This sector demands accountability.** It is the core work ethic. The work environment is structured, and you are responsible for delivering results to your team members and manager. This accountability ensures that your work has a direct and meaningful impact on the company's success.

Theoretical explorations vs. results-driven tasks

- **Academia:** As discussed earlier, academia involves conducting theoretical explorations to generate new knowledge in one's field.
- **Industry:** The industry relies on achieving specific results and meeting set goals. It operates in a highly result-driven environment. You are not performing well if your work does not produce the desired results.

Research methodology vs. product development cycles

- **Academia:** Academia allows you to use flexible research methodologies. Your professors can help you choose the most appropriate approach or methodology to complete your research. Additionally, you have the freedom to conduct in-depth investigations.
- **Industry:** The industry has strict cycles for product development. Your approaches are adjusted and tailored to meet the product's specific needs, ensuring deadlines are met and customer expectations are fulfilled. Clear deadlines and milestones are set to ensure the production of results.

Let's summarize the topic...

Key Takeaways
Academia

- Focus on theoretical research, exploration, and knowledge advancement.
- Measure success by the number of grants, publications, and depth of the study.
- Flexible timelines.

Industry

- Focus on practical applications and delivering real-world solutions.
- Measure success by KPIs, revenue generation, and customer satisfaction.
- fast-paced environment with tight deadlines

Performance Metrics in Academia & Industry

Success looks different when you're climbing the ladder towards the corporate world. In this section, we'll talk about performance metrics and what success looks like in academia and industry.

Performance Metrics Overview

You know it. Publications rule academia. The number of articles, citations, and secured grants is the traditional KPI in the academic field. Additionally, filing patents, training students, and making novel contributions to knowledge in a specific field are highly valued. In contrast, revenue, market share, and customer satisfaction take center stage in the corporate world.

Here's How Productivity and Success Work in Both Worlds

- **Academia:** In academia, productivity and success depend on the long-term vision. Research takes years since researchers aim to discover new things and generate new knowledge. Patience plays a key role here. In a nutshell, productivity and success are measured over time.
- **Industry: The** industry measures productivity and success in meeting quarterly and yearly goals, whether by achieving higher ROIs (return on investment) or retaining repeat customers.

Success Criterion Examination

Both academia and industry follow different paths when it comes to professional fulfillment. Each has its own success criteria.
Let's break them down below.

Tenure vs. promotion tracks

- **Academia:** Tenure in academia means job security for a set number of years, typically five or more. This stability allows you to focus on teaching, research, and publishing without worrying about job loss. For students, tenure is the period during which they complete their degrees and conduct research. Success in academia is measured by meeting these time-bound goals and achieving significant academic milestones. Your scholarly achievements, publications, and contributions to your field all define your success.
- **Industry:** In this sector, performance metrics and goal attainment drive career progression. It's not just about meeting your expectations, but about exceeding them. Have you boosted sales, improved KPIs, or brought unique skills? These accomplishments are the keys to promotion. Success in the industry is dynamic and measurable, often leading to greater autonomy and recognition. The industry rewards innovation, efficiency, and impactful results, propelling you toward higher positions and greater professional fulfillment.

Milestones and benchmarks

- **Academia:** Specific milestones mark your progress and success. These include publishing research in high-impact journals, securing grants for your projects, developing and launching new courses, and contributing to the academic community through conferences and collaborative research.
- **Industry:** Success is measured by benchmarks that vary depending on your field. These benchmarks include exceeding sales targets, successfully leading and completing major projects, demonstrating strong leadership skills, and possessing industry-specific expertise. Achieving these benchmarks proves your competence and enhances

your reputation and career prospects within your organization.

Key Takeaways

Academia:

- Productivity and success require a long-term vision.
- Securing more publications, or those of higher impact, and grants leads to greater success.
- Success means having job security or not having it.

Industry:

- Productivity and success depend on the company's quarterly or yearly goals.
- More KPIs lead to more success.
- Success relies on the number of goals you have achieved.

The Bottom Line:

This chapter sets the stage by providing an understanding of the basics of transitioning from academia to industry.

You can easily distinguish between academic and industrial realities, success metrics, and the mindset required to succeed in the corporate world.

Now that you have the picture, it's time to take action and start making changes to ensure a smooth transition.

In the upcoming chapter, we'll discuss how to be versatile in academia to achieve the best work performance in the industry.

* * *

Insights From People in Real Life

To make this a value-filled book, I have interviewed individuals to help you gain insights from those who have been through or are currently experiencing a transition.

Insights from Dr. Katrina Armstrong

Dr. Katrina Armstrong is a recent Ph.D. graduate in Physiology at the time of the interview. She is a perfect example of how recent graduates can transition into the industry.

During our discussion, she mentioned that while she's still working as a Research Assistant to publish her work, she's also actively seeking industry opportunities that align with her interests.

So, upon asking this question, **"How have you found the transition process so far?"**

She replied,

"Transitioning has been somewhat challenging, especially the networking aspect. I find digital networking platforms like LinkedIn to be more professional, and I prefer in-person interactions at conferences. However, I am adapting by expanding my networking efforts to include diverse events and seeking direct feedback on my applications to improve my approach."

Then, I asked, **"Given your networking challenges, what strategies are you employing to improve your connections?"**

To which she replied,

"I am broadening my network by attending conferences outside my direct field, such as a sports science conference in Colorado. I am also engaging more with local professional groups and participating

CHAPTER 1: UNDERSTANDING THE TRANSITION—ACADEMIA VS....

in events like Tech Tuesdays and Bioscience Association meetups in Winnipeg. These efforts are complemented by professional feedback on my resume to enhance my job applications."

Although I asked many more questions, here's another one with its answer:

What preparatory steps have you taken to prepare for this industry transition?

I have been exceptionally proactive, contacting industry professionals and completing relevant certifications, including a mini-MBA and an introduction to bioscience innovation course. These qualifications, coupled with webinars and conferences, are part of my strategy to stay informed and demonstrate my commitment to continuous learning.

In the end, **I asked her for some advice** that she would like to offer to people wanting or trying to transition, and she said,

"I recommend staying curious and open to learning. Understanding the various roles and functions within the industry is essential. Networking, taking additional courses, and engaging with alumni can provide significant insights and opportunities."

It is worth noting that by diligently following the guidance and insights Katrina shared in her interview, she successfully secured a notable industry position just before the publication of this book.

CHAPTER 2: Setting Yourself up for Versatility While in Academia

Versatility is an extra string to a player's bow. –Alex Oxlade-Chamberlain

The U.S. Bureau of Labour Statistics reports a 6.5% increase in employment from 2014 to 2024, indicating a higher demand for professionals in different industries (Preparing students for their futures: The role of higher education, 2023).

Consequently, due to the surge in opportunities, acquiring a position at a prestigious organization proves challenging without a solid professional background. While in academia, it's high time you set yourself up for versatility to make your profile stand out in the pool of applicants trying to secure that dream job.

Imagine a world where your skills are not limited to a single field but can be applied across various industries. This is the power of versatility. In this chapter, we will delve into the concept of versatility and how you can leverage it in academia to gain a better industry experience.

Let's get started!

Understanding Versatility and Identifying Opportunities for Growth

Research conducted by Harvard Business Review found that the COVID-19 pandemic puzzled and overwhelmed non-versatile leaders. In contrast, those with versatility and the capability to navigate unprecedented change coped well with the situation and excelled in their work environments (Robert B. (Rob) Kaiser et al., 2023).

Professionals aiming to enter the industry must possess not only knowledge but also a high degree of versatility.

Defining Versatility

Harvard Business Review defines versatility as the ability to foresee and react to change, and possessing a well-rounded collection of required behaviours and skills. They also state that versatility is the master ability to lead in this VUCA world, where VUCA stands for Volatility, Uncertainty, Complexity, and Ambiguity (Robert B. (Rob) Kaiser et al., 2023).

For instance, Lisa works as a copywriter in a medical firm. She is also knowledgeable about technology. She understands how to use email software to run and schedule campaigns. Therefore, if the email account manager goes on leave for any reason, the copywriter, Lisa, will easily fill the role to avoid any workflow problems. That's how versatility helps in a work setting.

Here's another example: Lucy studied Marketing in her bachelor's but took short courses in coding and web development. Her versatile skill set helped her land a job at a tech firm as a marketing specialist. Now, while she works on designing marketing campaigns for the firm, she also helps create web pages or offers little tweaks where needed, making her a valuable asset to the company.

Bringing Famous Personalities to the Table

If we turn back to the pages of history, we will see that even the most impactful personalities of the past were versatile. They weren't confined to one domain but had more abilities.

Below are some names (both from history and recent times) that possess versatile abilities:

- **Leonardo Da Vinci** was a Master of Engineering, art, and science. His skills enabled him to bridge gaps between disciplines and introduce innovative solutions.
- **Marissa Mayer:** She is the former CEO of Yahoo. From a search engine specialist to leading a large corporation, her versatility in transitioning between fields made her the best leader.
- **Steve Jobs:** Who doesn't know him? He's the founder of Apple. Although he is known for introducing advanced technology devices, his interests in design and aesthetics enabled him to create aesthetically appealing products, which fascinate the audience whenever he releases new products. As you can see, versatility also helps increase sales.

Have you met me? Lol.

I deem myself a force to be reckoned with, and I will give you a glimpse of my versatility in academia.

Meet Mary...

Throughout my academic journey, from my B.Sc. days to my current PhD program, I have been building a robust academic career while gaining invaluable experience outside the educational setting, demonstrating versatility and adaptability.

As an independent Home Comfort and Tax company contractor, I honed my communication and problem-solving skills. Engaging with diverse clients taught me empathy, the importance of customer satisfaction, and the value of swift and practical solutions.

Prior to these roles, I ventured into the entrepreneurial world, running my own hybrid business, Claretora Line, and working as a Sales and Marketing Executive for a sales company. This experience sharpened my strategic thinking and ability to manage multiple tasks efficiently. Balancing academia with entrepreneurship was challenging, but it enriched my understanding of business operations and client relations.

Volunteering has always been close to my heart, and I have actively participated in various volunteer activities. Whether facilitating lab events for young students, participating in health awareness programs, or mentoring students, I believe in giving back to the community.

These experiences have allowed me to develop strong leadership and mentoring skills. Engaging in activities beyond research and teaching has equipped me with a well-rounded skill set, making me a more effective researcher, educator, and professional.

This journey highlights the importance of exploring and capitalizing on the numerous resources and opportunities available in both academic and non-academic settings.

Did I mention the myriad resources and opportunities in the academic setting? Yes, I did! Contrary to the widespread belief that academia stifles personal development and limits professional versatility, my journey through academic institutions has revealed a wealth of resources designed to foster growth and adaptability.

These resources, however, are not handed to you on a silver platter; you must actively seek them out and take advantage of what academia has to offer.

Hidden Gems in Academia

While the primary focus of academic life may seem to be research and teaching, educational institutions offer numerous opportunities for personal and professional growth. These opportunities come in various forms, including:

- **Free training courses:** Academic institutions often offer workshops and classes on a wide range of topics, from advanced research techniques to soft skills like communication and leadership. These courses are typically free for staff and students and can be a valuable addition to your skill set.
- **Certifications:** Many academic institutions partner with professional organizations to offer certification programs. These certifications can enhance your qualifications and boost your competitiveness in the job market.
- **Personal development programs:** Academic institutions often organize seminars, conferences, and guest lectures that offer insights into various fields and career paths. These events are excellent for networking and broadening your horizons.
- **Mentorship and Community Engagement**: Academia offers various mentorship programs and community engagement opportunities that contribute to personal growth.

Reflecting on my experiences, I have benefited immensely from these resources. For instance, during my time at the University of Manitoba, I attended numerous workshops that sharpened my research skills and gave me a deeper understanding of advanced scientific techniques.

I also discovered and took advantage of their career mentor program for students. I was paired with a career mentor professional in my field of interest and had the opportunity to conduct informational interviews with them.

The career services help you prepare and tailor your cover letter and resume for jobs you are interested in.

Additionally, I participated in personal development and project seminars, as well as lab-organized journal clubs, which helped me improve my public speaking and presentation skills. These skills are crucial in both academia and industry.

One of the seminars was where I met, networked, and connected with Reuben Saba, an industry professional whom I interviewed for this book.

- **Taking initiative:** The key to unlocking these opportunities is initiative. Academia will not spoon-feed you these resources; you must proactively seek them out.
- **Staying Informed:** Regularly check your university's bulletin boards, websites, and newsletters for upcoming courses and event announcements.
- **Networking:** Engage with colleagues, mentors, and advisors who can point you toward valuable opportunities and resources.
- **Setting goals:** Identify areas where you want to grow and actively seek resources that can help you achieve your goals.

In conclusion, academia is far from a dead end regarding personal and professional development. It is a vibrant environment filled with opportunities for those willing to look for them. By taking the initiative, you can make the most of what academia offers and prepare yourself for a successful transition to industry or any other professional field.

Type of Skills Required to Adopt Versatility

It entirely depends on your interests when it comes to acquiring more skills; however, here are the types of skills that are must-haves for anyone thinking of transitioning to the industry and nailing the position:

- **Technical skills:** You should know how to use tools, software, or other technical methodologies relevant to your field before moving to the industry.
- **Transferable skills:** Skills like communication, problem-solving, teamwork, and critical thinking apply to all industries, so these are must-haves!
- **Soft skills** encompass a range of interpersonal abilities, including time management, leadership, emotional intelligence, and other essential competencies. To excel in the corporate world, these are essential.

Growth Opportunities Versatility Has to Offer

Versatility offers a myriad of opportunities, both in personal and professional lives. Here are some areas where versatility can unlock your potential:

Professional Advancement

- **More value in the job market:** If you have a versatile skill set, you become an attractive candidate for the company's HR department. Furthermore, it enables you to apply to various positions, demonstrating your adaptability and increasing your chances of acceptance.

- **Leadership potential:** Being versatile allows for a broader perspective, enables you to think critically, and can help you be more effective in problem-solving. These are skills necessary for a leader, and consequently, they give you an advantage in securing leadership roles within the company.
- **Career flexibility:** In case you find the industry you joined unfulfilling, versatility allows you to switch careers and move to an area that interests you. So, versatility lets you explore different roles throughout your professional journey.
- **Upskilling and reskilling**: Versatility allows you to have a growth mindset. Therefore, while working or studying, you strive to learn more skills in your arsenal and become future-proof in the job market.

Personal Advancement

- **Problem-solving ability:** You become able to be creative and provide practical solutions as an individual.
- **Increased confidence:** Having more skills and knowledge gives you greater confidence in yourself, exuding a powerful personality that consistently impresses others.
- **Lifelong learning:** You develop a continuous learning mindset. Seeking new knowledge and experiences keeps you motivated and productive, while also fostering adaptability and intellectual growth.
- **Network expansion:** When you learn new skills, you meet new people, make new friends, and ultimately expand your network, which is a win-win!

Strategies to Cultivate Versatility in Academia

You can cultivate versatility in several ways while pursuing an academic career.

Here are some key strategies to do so:

Engage in Work and Internships

- **Look out for relevant work experience:** Fake it till you make it. In academia, try to find internships that help you work in a professional setting and gain real-world experience. If internships aren't available, consider part-time jobs. If time constraints or other reasons make part-time jobs challenging, explore freelance opportunities. These options aim to enhance your resume, gain practical knowledge, and contribute to your professional development while working.
- **Balancing work and study:** Effective time management is crucial for maintaining a versatile profile. Therefore, as you study and work simultaneously, focus on learning to manage your time effectively to succeed in both areas.

Volunteer and Get Involved in the Community

While in academia, if you're not employed, make an effort to volunteer and actively participate in your community.

Here are some benefits to it:
You get the chance to,

- develop soft skills,
- build networks,

- Build your resume,
- and become the preferred candidate.

Types of Volunteering

There are many options to explore and join as a volunteer, aligning with your interests.

For instance, joining non-profit organizations, participating in community events, or holding student government positions can provide you with the best volunteer experiences.

Take Short Courses and Certifications

Taking short courses and certifications can significantly enhance your skills and versatility..

Here's a roadmap to enroll in courses and acquire certifications to build a well-rounded skill set.:

- **Identify valuable courses:** Research and learn about all the short courses, certifications, or boot camps that complement your industry requirements.
- **Balance coursework and additional learning:** Take time to study your courses. Manage your time and prioritize tasks to balance academic work and further learning effectively.
- **Highlight certifications:** After completing your short courses and certifications, add them to your resume and discuss them during interviews.

Build a Professional Network

You already know how networking helps you become more versatile.

Here are some strategies to develop an excellent professional network:

- Use online platforms like LinkedIn and connect with experienced professionals in your relevant industry.
- Attend industry events, conferences, and workshops to connect with people.
- Participate in career fairs and alums events organized by your university. Volunteering for these events would be an added benefit.
- Reach out to professionals and conduct interviews to learn about their career paths and gain valuable tips for your professional journey.

Assessing Your Current Skills

It's time to help you understand your position. The initial step to achieving versatility is recognizing your strengths and weaknesses.

The following are some steps to assess yourself:

What skills have you developed through research, writing, and academic presentations? List them below.

_____
_____
_____
_____
_____

Reflect on extracurricular activities you participated in through-

out your academic career. Identify the leadership roles you participated in, problems you solved, and more. Write them below.

_____
_____
_____
_____
_____

Evaluate your soft skills, including interpersonal skills, time management, and more, as these are crucial for industry success. Write them.

_____
_____
_____
_____
_____

List all the technical skills you currently possess. For instance, write down your software proficiency, data analytical skills, or any other tools you have used before.

_____
_____
_____
_____
_____

Analyzing your skills thoroughly will help you determine which skills are already in your toolkit and identify which additional skills to acquire. Next, compile the list and begin taking courses, reading books, and exploring online tutorials to enhance your professional profile.

Learning Skills To Be Versatile

As explained earlier, you need to learn three types of skills to become versatile. It's time to help you with the "how!"

Learning Technical Skills

In this digital world, technical skills can open new doors to exciting job opportunities.

Here are some steps to acquire technical skills:

- The first step is determining what technical skills are in demand in your desired industry. You can do this by hopping onto LinkedIn, Indeed, or Glassdoor and checking out the job descriptions to see what technical skills employers are looking for in their candidates.
- Now, look for certifications or short courses from your college/university's departments to help you learn your desired technical skills.
- Platforms like Coursera, edX, Udemy, and others offer a wide variety of paid and unpaid courses in various technical skills, including coding, data analysis, and project management.
- There are also many skill-specific platforms. For instance, if you want to learn programming/coding, you can go to Codecademy or DataCamp.
- Lastly, YouTube is the best resource for learning. There, you can watch many courses and tutorials shared by experts for free.

Learning Transferable Skills

Transferable skills are the backbone of versatility. You can utilize these skills in many industries and come across as a versatile professional.

Here's how to learn and develop transferable skills like leadership, time management, problem-solving, teamwork, and more:

- **Discover your strengths.** Learn what transferable skills you already possess and have demonstrated in the past. List them below.

_____
_____
_____
_____
_____

- Participate in class discussions, presentations, and group projects to encourage open communication and enhance critical thinking.
- Take on leadership roles in your university or other settings to learn how to lead effectively.
- Seek help from online courses.
- Become an active listener during conversations with your colleagues.
- Continuously ask for feedback from your colleagues and friends on your performance when demonstrating these skills.
- Challenge yourself by engaging in public speaking to enhance confidence.

Learning Soft Skills

As discussed above, soft skills encompass a range of abilities, including communication skills, interpersonal skills, and others. Learning them is also pretty easy. You can follow the next-mentioned strategies to add soft skills to your arsenal:

- Start active listening and improve your communication skills. Let people know you're paying attention.
- Every interaction, written or verbal, is your chance to practice communication skills. Utilize that.
- Take courses and learn about these skills.
- Pay attention to how you respond to things and work on improving.
- Become a mentor and guide others while developing your interpersonal skills.
- Read and read more books.
- Volunteer and work in teams to learn where to improve and become a better professional.

Prepare for Transition

Now that you have thoroughly learned how to become a versatile leader in academia, it's time to implement what you have learned and prepare for the transition.

Here's how you can prepare for the transition:

Set Goals

Set goals and define your long-term career goals. List out three short-term and three long-term goals.

Short-Term Goals

_____
_____
_____
_____
_____

Long-Term Goals

_____
_____
_____
_____
_____

Create Milestones

Create small milestones to achieve those goals and work towards them. Write them here:

_____
_____
_____
_____
_____

Update Your Resume

Utilize your time in academia effectively. Update your resume with all the experiences you've previously had and add more while you work or do internships in your industry.

Benefit From the University Services

Leverage the career services provided by educational institutions to seek guidance.

Document and Reflect on Experiences

As you work towards your goals and prepare to transition into the industry, document the entire process. This documentation could be beneficial in the future or serve as a guide for anyone who may need help in the future. It could also serve as a great portfolio.

You can create your experience portfolio using this worksheet:

Categorize Your Experiences

Category	Description	Write Here
Academic Work	Courses, research projects, presentations, awards, publications	
Volunteer Work	Activities where you provided services without expecting compensation	
Internships	Positions held within an organization for a specific period	
Projects	Independent creations, group projects, and competitions	

Analyze Each Experience

Analyze each experience by filling out the following sheet (you will find a few extra sheets like this one at the end of this book):

Title: _____

_____

Organization/Institution: _____

_____

Start Date: _____

_____

End Date: _____

_____

Description: _____

_____
_____
_____
_____

Skills Used:

_____
_____
_____
_____
_____

Accomplishments:

_____
_____
_____
_____
_____

Portfolio Planning

Format

Will it be physical or digital?

Target Audience

Who is going to be the target audience of your portfolio? Potential employers, graduate schools, etc.

Content Selection

Review the experiences listed above and choose ones to add to your portfolio that align with the requirements of your target audience and career goals.

Presentation

Think about how you will present your work in your portfolio. Will you use clear visuals, concise writing, a user-friendly layout, or something else?

The Bottom Line

Let's face it. Becoming versatile is an ongoing journey that requires continuous learning, actively seeking experiences, building a strong network, and much more.

Remember that versatility is not limited to having a collection of skills but also about using them to tackle challenges in your personal and professional lives.

So, as Stephen R. Covey says in his book, 7 Habits of Highly Effective

People, "Begin with the end in mind" and take the first step towards versatility and, ultimately, a bright future.

Appendices

Resources

Books

- "So Good They Can't Ignore You: Why Skills Trump Passion in the Real World" by Cal Newport
- "Mindset: The New Psychology of Success" by Carol Dweck
- "Versatility: How to Optimize Interactions When 7 Workplace Behaviours Are at Their Worst" by Francie Dalton

Podcasts:

- Portfolio Career Podcast with David Nebinski
- The Knowledge Project with Shane Parrish
- The Tim Ferriss Show with Tim Ferriss
- EntreLeadership with Ramsey Network

* * *

Insights From Samuel Ogunsola

Samuel Ogunsola is a fourth-year PhD student in the Department of Physiology at the time of the interview. His research focuses on splicing mechanisms in health and genetic diseases. He transitioned to this PhD program in 2022 from a master's program within the same department; he is also honoured to have been named a 2023 Vanier Scholar. His passions extend beyond the lab, including leadership and engaging in innovative business and community development projects.

During my interview with him, I asked him the following questions, which might be helpful to you:

Are you considering a transition to industry, and if so, what motivates you?

"Yes, I am exploring opportunities in both industry and consulting. I consider three main factors in my career decisions: assets, aspirations, and market needs. My PhD has equipped me with skills in leadership, project management, marketing, and sales. I aspire to find a role that allows me to balance my professional goals with personal commitments, such as running my non-profit organization and spending time with my family. My skills would be highly applicable in industry and consulting roles."

Which skills are most valuable for transitioning to industry?

"Project management and the ability to work under pressure are invaluable. Managing my research projects independently has honed my project management skills, making them transferable to any industry setting. The fast-paced nature of my research has also prepared me well for the industry's dynamic environment."

What advice would you give fellow graduate students considering

moving to industry?

1. "Focus on building a diverse skill set and aim high.
2. Market yourself effectively and pursue roles that align with your aspirations.
3. Remember, your career does not define you; strive to be **adaptable** and **versatile** across various settings."

Can you recommend any specific resources or books?
"A robust LinkedIn profile is essential. Books such as Reid Hoffman's The Startup of You, Carol Dweck's Mindset, James Clear's Atomic Habits, and Napoleon Hill's Think and Grow Rich have greatly influenced my personal and professional development."

CHAPTER 3: Creating Your Brand

> *Your brand is what sets you apart from others. It's what makes you unique and memorable.* –Michael Hyatt

Your brand is your ticket to the corporate world. As you transition from the academic landscape to the industry, having a personal brand makes it significantly easier.

It is a foolproof tool for success. By acting as an elevator pitch, your brand communicates your skills, experiences, and value propositions without requiring effort to reach potential employers.

I call it the essential tool for evolving your career and standing out in this competitive job market. In this chapter, I will help you assess your current self and equip you with the required knowledge and strategies to build a powerful personal brand that resonates with your relevant industry.

So, let's get into it without further ado!

Self-Assessment: Know Yourself

Building a solid personal brand begins with understanding yourself. Identify your interests, qualities, expectations, challenges, skills, experiences, and offerings to establish a solid foundation for your brand.

So, let's begin the journey of self-discovery. You have already assessed your skill set in the previous chapter. Grab that paper and reread it, this time with the perspective of considering them as the abilities that make you who you are!

After that, bridge the gaps by charting a course to build a strong narrative for your brand.

Here's a quick questionnaire to help you understand yourself before you create your brand. Write answers to all of these questions to reveal your inner compass!

Interests and Values

- **What are you curious about?** Write things that spark your interest and motivate you.

_____
_____
_____
_____
_____

- **What are your core values?** Write down the principles that hold great value in your life, such as creativity, honesty, loyalty, or innovation. By aligning your values with your brand, you can discover your authentic self.

_____
_____
_____
_____
_____

- **What inspires you?** Write down who your role models are. What are the causes that provoke you to take action?

_____
_____
_____
_____
_____

Skills and Experiences

- **What are you naturally good at?** List your skills.

_____
_____
_____
_____
_____

- **What experiences have shaped your skills?** Document all academic, co-curricular, and other experiences that have shaped your development.

_____
_____
_____
_____
_____

- **What are your proudest achievements?** List your awards, successes in academic projects, or anything that made you feel proud about yourself.

_____
_____
_____
_____
_____

Expectations and Challenges

- **What are your long-term goals?** Write down your aspirations and goals for the next five to ten years.

_____
_____
_____
_____
_____

- **What is your ideal work environment?** Identify the office atmosphere and environment that best suits your skills and preferences.

_____
_____
_____
_____
_____

- **What do you think are your roadblocks to building a solid personal brand?** Time constraints? Self-doubt? Do you need guidance on using social media?

CHAPTER 3: CREATING YOUR BRAND

_____
_____
_____
_____
_____

Value Proposition: The Most Crucial One

- What skills and experiences can help your potential employers/dream company?

_____
_____
_____
_____
_____

- What problems can you solve for your employers?

_____
_____
_____
_____
_____

- How can your brand contribute to a larger purpose and cause?

_____
_____
_____
_____

Bonus Section

- Write down three words that describe your personality.

_____
_____
_____
_____
_____

- Think of your ideal employer or dream company and brainstorm what qualities they will appreciate in you.

_____
_____
_____
_____
_____

Remember!

- Nothing is right or wrong. Everything you have listed until now makes you the best version of yourself. So, accept yourself as you are and take pride in who you are.
- These answers are just the beginning. I'll guide you throughout the process to help you become an impactful personal brand.
- Use the insights above to create a unique brand message that resonates with your employers/dream companies.

CHAPTER 3: CREATING YOUR BRAND

Now that you have listed answers to all these questions and are self-aware, it's time to begin working on your brand. Remember, this brand will be your guiding light, attracting numerous opportunities to create a fulfilling journey.

Boost Your Online Presence

In today's technological world, having a strong online presence enables you to create a powerful personal brand that has an impact in both the digital and real worlds.

Employers might search for you online, and if they see a strong profile online, they may even hire you without a second thought.

So, let's help you build a strong online presence—the first step toward establishing your brand.

- Create your space on different digital platforms. **LinkedIn** is the best platform for professionals like yourself.
- **Optimize** your profile. Create an irresistible headline and an impressive author bio. Describe your skills, experiences, and awards in detail. Ensure you use keywords related to your industry to increase your visibility in search engines.
- Create an **online portfolio** on a professional website. You can add projects you have previously worked on. Your publications and work samples should also be there.
- **Connect** with successful professionals online to introduce yourself. Share relevant insights while engaging with their posts.

Edit Your Resume for Industry Roles

A resume works as an unpaid brand ambassador for you. Creating a good resume is a great marketing tool for job applications. So, when applying for jobs or internships, tailor your resume for every job you apply for.

- Highlight the skills they are looking for in their ideal candidate.
- Incorporate keywords from their job description.
- Ensure your resume passes the ATS (Applicant Tracking System), which many companies use to filter out resumes.
- Outline your work experiences more concisely and highlight your achievements more prominently in your resume to make a better impression.
- Keep it concise and to the point.

Creating Your Brand

After successfully understanding your capabilities and setting your profile, it's time to work on your brand. Let's take a strategic approach to building a solid personal brand that not only targets your desired audience but also demonstrates your unique value proposition.

Defining Your Unique Value Proposition

A unique value proposition is a sentence that clearly defines the benefits of your products and services to the target audience, providing solutions to their needs. The statement also helps differentiate you from your competition.

It would be beneficial to have a clear and distinct value proposition to establish your brand. Answer the following questions before creating your UVP:

What Makes You Unique?

_____
_____
_____

Who Is Your Target Audience?

_____
_____
_____

What Are Their Pain Points?

_____
_____
_____

What Are Your Strengths?

_____
_____
_____

How Can You Benefit Your Readers?

_____
_____
_____

Time to Craft Your UVP

You should follow the following structure to create your UVP (as it's the standard format used by many):

I help **[add your target audience]** achieve **[whatever outcome your target audience desires]** by **[mention your unique strength/ability/solution to their problem]**.

For example,

I help **marketing managers in the health industry** create **compelling marketing campaigns** to **drive traffic through irresistible social media strategies.**

Now, write your UVP here:

_____
_____
_____

Refine Your UVP and Test

After creating the first draft of your UVP, do these final things:

- Refine it by getting it reviewed by your mentors, advisors, or friends.
- Ensure the statement resonates with your audience's problems.
- Ensure the statement offers what they are looking for

Having done it all, test your UVP by sharing it with your audience through ads or simply as a headline on your professional profile. If it gets you results, well and good. Otherwise, find errors and create it again.

Fun fact: You can always change your UVP as you gain new experiences and add more skills to your toolbox.

How to Launch Your Brand

Having a strong UVP ready is not enough. It's time to market yourself. Here's what you need to do to launch your brand and create a strong brand image:

Prioritize Authenticity and Transparency

Generic slogans are big turn-offs. Don't opt for overused words for your slogan, but focus on what truly defines your motto and what makes your brand unique.

Here's what you need to do to create your brand logo:

1. **Values first:** Think of your core values. They can be honesty, loyalty, or anything that you value and want to offer your audience.
2. **Goal power:** Think of what goal you want to achieve through your brand. For instance, a successful author's goal can be to help 100 writers get their stories published.
3. **Time for wordplay:** Now, you have to find rhyming words that help create your brand's slogan. For instance, "Finger Licking' Good" or "Dream Big, Climb High!" Create something like these for your brand!

Keep It Precise

Now, go ahead and write your slogans. Aim for 5-7 words. Stay within this limit so your audience remembers the slogan.

Write down the final versions.

Check If It's Unique

Now, finalize one and check if it's unique. Does it reflect *your* true self?

Test Drive!

It's time to get it checked by friends and mentors and ask them if your slogan leaves a lasting impression. If they approve, this is it!

Once you have completed the slogan, it's time to share your story. Be transparent and share your story with your audience in a way that sparks their interest.

Here's a guide on creating your brand with transparency

Foundation of honesty

- **Be authentic:** Remember to stay true to yourself and genuine when sharing your story. Don't be afraid to include details about your past mistakes. Beginning from the origin to where you are right now, write about it all without the fear of being judged.
- **Have clear values:** Keeping your life principles in mind, write something that reflects your core values in your story. Share with your audience the values that guide your decisions and actions.

Show them your process

- **Don't tell, show:** Share the process behind delivering your products and services. Show them your work ethic, team dynamics, production process, or anything that reveals what goes on behind the scenes.
- **Develop a human connection:** Show them the human force behind your brand. Tell them the real-life stories and experiences of people behind your brand's image.

Take customer feedback

- **Ask for feedback:** Request feedback from customers who have previously received your services or products, and feature them on your website or social media. It will significantly impact your success, as people tend to believe in word of mouth. So, gather as much feedback as you can. Add this feedback to your brand story as well.

Highlight your impact and sustainability

- **Go beyond profit:** Your brand story should convey to your audience that you value commitment and responsibility. Show them how responsibly you carry out your processes and deliver to your customers.
- **Be transparent:** Share every detail of your work ethic with them, so they trust you.

Show them your imperfections

- **Nobody's perfect:** Remember, nobody's perfect. Everybody makes mistakes, and you should not be ashamed of them. Talk about the mistakes you have made in your brand story and tell them how you

learned from them.
- **Focus on your progress:** Tell them how you've progressed from scratch to where you stand today. Share with them your efforts, struggles, challenges, and successes in your story so that they can relate to it.

Bonus Tip

Craft your story, aligning it with your audience's interests: Consider what aspects of your story will have the most significant impact on your audience and discuss them. Discuss your audience's interests and keep your story relevant to them.

Networking and Career Advancement Through Personal Branding

Personal branding is not only about your digital presence or a good resume; it's about how your audience perceives and connects with you.

Your brand should work as a magnet, attracting people and helping you advance your career.

Here's how you can leverage your brand:

- **Networking:** Your brand is a magnet. Use it to attract industry leaders, employers, and other professionals you think would benefit your growth. Connect with them through various conferences, gatherings, and other events.
- **Building relationships:** Engage in conversations that develop relationships with other professionals. Don't just stay at the talking stage; showcase a deep interest in their story while telling your own.
- **Job search:** When searching for a job, incorporate your personal

brand's messaging or UVP in your cover letter or resume to stand out in the crowd and capture their attention.
- **Be consistent:** Maintain a consistent brand image. Whether you're job searching, posting on your social media accounts, or engaging in person conversations, it's crucial to promote your brand. This approach will contribute to your brand's growth and leave a lasting impression on your audience.

The Bottom Line

Creating a personal brand requires constant effort. You must continue to provide value to your audience and continually develop your skills to reap benefits from your brand in the corporate world.

Use the worksheets in this chapter to make an impact on your audience and to transition smoothly from academia to industry. It's time to make yourself a brand!

* * *

Insights From Reuben Saba

Can you briefly introduce yourself and describe your current role in the industry?

"My name is Reuben Saba. I am the Vice President of Business Development for Medicure and its subsidiaries in the U.S. I started as a medical science liaison and progressed to Director of Medical Affairs, overseeing medical information and liaison activities. Eventually, I became the Vice President of Medical Affairs and Business Affairs and initiated the business development unit at Medicure. This role spans contracting, operations, market access, patents, and legal aspects in the U.S. Currently, my focus is primarily on business development."

That's quite a transition from academia to industry. Can you share what your research focused on during your academic days and what motivated you to pursue it?

"I started with a master's degree in microbiology but shifted to medical microbiology due to my lack of interest in industrial applications. I completed my PhD at the National Microbiology Lab, focusing on prion diseases. This project was particularly challenging as it was a new study area. Early in my PhD, inspired by Nobel Prize-winning research in gene expression, I proposed studying the role of non-coding RNA in prion diseases. My principal investigator supported this innovative approach, and I developed the first microRNA microarray, leading to a paper referenced over 5,000 times. This paper significantly influenced my P.I.'s research direction, incorporating it into her main program."

You were deeply involved in your research. However, you seem to like constant change and growth, which is impressive. At what point did you start considering a transition to industry?

"I thrive on constant changes and added responsibilities that directly impact me. I want my efforts to have a tangible impact rather than just being a document on a shelf; I aim for them to effect real change.

"I always had an eye on the industry. During my PhD, I collaborated with companies such as Roche and Ambion, now part of Thermo Fisher, to secure samples and products for my research. This proactive engagement put me on their radar, and they began contacting me for product evaluations. Additionally, having a family member in the industry provided opportunities for collaboration and access to advanced equipment, further aligning my academic work with industry applications."

How did you transition from academia to industry?

"After completing a postdoc in Germany and returning to work with the government, I found the changing mandates and lack of support in science motivating me to seek new challenges in the industry. My transition was facilitated by my readiness to embrace challenges and step out of my comfort zone. I started as a medical science liaison in the industry, quickly moving up due to my ability to adapt and take on new responsibilities."

Are there specific resources you would recommend to students considering a transition from academia to industry?

"While I can't recommend specific books, being active in industry-related societies and networking within these groups is invaluable. These connections can open doors and provide insights not typically accessible through academic channels alone."

CHAPTER 4: Networking and Mentorship: Building Your Industry Connections

Your network is your net worth. –Porter Gale

Jason, a recent graduate in mass communication, is passionate about becoming a public speaker. However, he lacks industry experience and needs assistance in his field.

One day, he woke up, scrolled through LinkedIn, and mustered the courage to reach out to industry professionals. He sent seven messages to the top Gs of his industry.

Guess what? One out of seven responded to his message, stating that she was ready to conduct an informational interview with him. That person was a successful mindset speaker who guides people on controlling their minds to stay calm and productive.

Jason was surprised that she agreed to provide advice on how to speak in public.

Anyway, Jason interviewed her, took her advice, and mentioned his aspiration to become a public speaker. She connected him with a potential employer looking for a public speaker. This connection helped Jason start his professional life in the industry.

You see how networking helped Jason change the course of his life. If he hadn't sent connection requests on LinkedIn, he would have struggled to advance his career.

80% of the professionals interviewed in this book came through networking. I used to think I was terrible at networking, but I took a big step and started trying. I usually tell myself, "What's the worst that could happen? No one will be mean to me. I'll either get a yes or a no, or they'll ignore me." But no matter what happens, someone will reach out to me. I also received numerous rejections when I attempted to reach out to professionals for this book. But here I am, and networking changed everything.

Networking almost always changes everything. Your network is what makes you (your net worth)—Porter Gale's quote. The professional world depends on making connections and thriving through them.

In this tough job market, your network can help you get invaluable opportunities. This chapter will discuss how to establish a strong network through alum networks, how to conduct compelling interviews, and how to foster meaningful relationships. We'll also learn about mentorship and how it can help you succeed.

What is the Power of Networks?

The power of a network lies in its ability to provide you with connections, resources, and opportunities. It serves as a springboard, helping you in various ways to grow and advance your professional career.

- **Your network provides access to knowledge and expertise:** If you have individuals with experience and knowledge in your field within your network, you gain access to all their knowledge and expertise. You learn from their experiences and copy the blueprint.
- **Your network offers numerous opportunities, providing several benefits.** More associations will provide more job opportunities and, ultimately, success in your career.
- **Your network enhances your credibility and visibility.** If you're part of a network, your credibility increases as more people

learn about your expertise and the things you do. Ultimately, you become an attractive candidate to employers.
- **Your network offers mutual support and collaboration:** You develop a sense of belonging by building strong connections. You can seek guidance and support from experts in your network and offer assistance to those who need it.
- **Your network offers lifelong learning:** Networking provides an opportunity to continuously learn as you interact with individuals from diverse career stages, gaining insights into their experiences and expertise.

How Do You Leverage Alumni Networks and Professional Associations

Imagine stepping into a room full of professionals who share your alma mater and your fervent passion for your chosen field. This profound sense of belonging, nurtured by your extensive alum network, whether from the academic or industrial spheres, is an invaluable asset that can substantially enhance your chances of success.

Here's a detailed explanation of how alum networks and professional associations help provide you with insights and opportunities in the corporate world:

- **Stronger bond due to shared background**
- **Events and platforms for expansion**
- **Expert guidance**
- **Resources and job postings**

How Do Informational Interviews Help in Gaining Industry Insight?

Informational interviews offer valuable insights into the career paths of successful professionals. They offer a treasure trove of benefits to young and aspiring professionals.

Here are some benefits of conducting informational interviews:

- You gain direct access to professionals in your industry and can obtain firsthand information from them, rather than conducting research online or reading books.
- You can inquire about their journey from a novice to an expert. What was the entire job process? How were they interviewed? What were the employers' expectations? And how did they manage to overcome all these challenges?
- By asking the right questions, you can gain insights into a company's culture, work environment, and team dynamics. This information will help you determine which company aligns best with your needs and expectations.
- Informational interviews are a journey of discovery. You'll learn about the latest industry trends and in-demand skills, gaining a deeper understanding of your field and sparking excitement for your career development. It's like possessing the secret code to excel in your industry's exam!
- Lastly, you develop good relationships with experienced professionals in your industry and have the opportunity to connect with them. And the best part? They might connect you with valuable people in their network to help you grow!

How to Conduct Informational Interviews?

To conduct compelling interviews with successful professionals in your industry, follow specific steps. I have mentioned them below:

1. **Know "who" you want to interview**

- **Industry research:** You know your desired industry, right? Use the internet to research successful professionals. Make a list of those you think can be helpful. It will prepare you for the next steps. Remember that there are many opportunities and different job descriptions, so be open to exploring and researching niches related to your desired interest. You will be surprised by the variety of job roles available. Then go ahead and learn about these roles in your informational interview.
- **Refine your list:** Reach out to those you see as credible in your niche.

1. **Create a personalized message**

- **Introduce yourself professionally:** Ensure you introduce yourself professionally when writing a message. Share your work or education status and your aspirations.
- **Mention your purpose clearly:** Clearly state your purpose and why you are contacting them. Avoid unnecessary fluff.
- **Offer flexibility:** Inform them that you have multiple time slots available for the interview, allowing them to choose or suggest a time that suits them best.

Templates Samples

Greetings, [Their Name]!

I am [Your Name], a [Your Current Professional Status—for instance, a recent graduate of mass communication and an aspiring public speaker].

I'm highly impressed by your work and expertise in [Mention Their Field]. I'm interested in learning more about the industry and your career path, such as what skills are in demand.

I would greatly appreciate the opportunity to learn from your experience through this interview. Your insights would be invaluable to me.

I'm available to chat/ call at [Mention Time Slots] at your convenience. Let me know if you'd like to connect with me.

Thank you for your time and consideration.

Sincerely,

[Your Name]

Prepare thoughtful queries

- **Career journey:** Ask them about their journey, the challenges they encountered, the skills they acquired, and any insider tips they can share.
- **Industry insights:** Ask about current industry trends, their outlook on the future, and the most in-demand skills for success.
- **Company culture:** Learn about the company's culture, inquire about its work environment, and discover what employees enjoy most about their jobs.
- **Career advice:** Seek their guidance on navigating the job market and securing a win. Inquire about the roadmap to success in the position.

Show your appreciation

- After interviewing them and asking all the questions, express your gratitude and convey your appreciation for their time. You can also briefly summarize the key takeaways from the conversation if you'd like.
- **Follow-up:** Maintain the connection with them by following up. Share your progress or let them know your plans to stay in touch and keep them in your contact list.

Insider Tip: Show them that you respect their time.

Time to Enhance Your Networking Skills

A strong network is a cornerstone of your career's success. It opens multiple doors for you, but the art of networking is a fundamental skill. Yes, it's more than attending conferences and events, and offering business cards.

The following are some key strategies to master networking:

Be an Active Listener

Active listening is the cornerstone of effective communication. By attentively listening to the speaker, you instantly win their heart. Additionally, actively listening to others' stories fosters the development of strong relationships.

Ask clarifying questions to demonstrate your genuine interest in what they have to say. By actively listening to their perspectives and experiences, you gain valuable insights and learn from their knowledge and expertise. Ultimately, an active listener leaves a lasting impression on the speaker.

Learn How To Start a Conversation

The majority of people, particularly introverts, struggle to initiate conversations. However, I've compiled some strategies to help you gather the courage and begin conversations that can expand your network. Here's what you need to do to start a conversation:

- **Prepare conversation starter words/phrases:** Before approaching them, make sure you have a good conversation starter. Avoid asking generic questions like, "What do you do?" Instead, conduct some research and discuss their achievements or ask about industry trends that interest you.
- **Talk about your passions and interests:** Don't be afraid to share your passions with others. Express what you love to do or what you aspire to achieve. Your passions might resonate with their experiences, and they could offer valuable guidance and support.
- **Keep your focus on quality conversations:** Ensure that the conversation remains meaningful and engaging. Avoid sharing trivial details like eating a salad in the morning (unless they are interested in healthy eating), as they may not find it particularly interesting.

Know the Power of Your Body Language

- Your body language conveys a great deal, so it's essential to be mindful when interacting with people you want to expand your professional network. Here are some tips to project a powerful body language:

- Maintain eye contact.
- Give them a genuine smile.
- Keep your posture active.
- Demonstrate confidence through your body language.
- Avoid fidgeting, as it can make them think you're confused.
- Show enthusiasm.
- Make them feel genuinely interested through gestures.

Insider Tip: *Remember that your positive energy is contagious to like-minded people, so express it to develop connections with them.*

Following up Is the Key

When you meet someone new, take the time to send them a thank-you note as soon as you leave the venue. This simple gesture demonstrates your appreciation and helps you maintain a positive connection. You can also mention something you particularly enjoyed about the meeting in the note.

Make Use of Social Media Platforms

To develop a strong network, ensure you're active on social media platforms, particularly LinkedIn. Add relevant keywords to your profile to increase its visibility when employers search for industry professionals.

Additionally, consider joining groups related to your industry to share knowledge and gain valuable insights. This approach positions you as a thought leader, attracting more potential employers, particularly in your field.

Warm Introductions Are Powerful

You can ask them if they know any friends, colleagues, or mentors in your industry so that you can connect with them. Remember, a warm introduction can help you connect with someone new and make the situation less awkward.

Give Back to Your Network

Giving and taking are universal principle that works in various aspects of life. When constructing a network to gain support, opportunities, and advice, it's important to remember that some individuals may also require your assistance. By sharing your experiences and insights with those who are less experienced than you, you can create a strong support system that will benefit both of you (they become your support system).

Be Authentic and Genuine

Be authentic and don't try to be someone you're not. Embrace your true self and let your personality stand out in every interaction. Remember, trust is the foundation of reliability.

Practice! Practice!! Practice!!!

Practice makes perfect. So, if you're new to networking, don't be afraid to step out of your comfort zone. It's okay to make mistakes; everything improves with consistent effort. Continue practicing, and eventually, you'll build a strong network that'll undoubtedly be beneficial when you enter the corporate world.

Mentorship and Career Success?

While focusing on networking with like-minded individuals, it's equally important to connect with industry leaders and seek mentorship.

A mentor is a trusted advisor who provides support, guidance, and advice as you navigate your career path. Therefore, it's crucial to find a suitable mentor for yourself.

Here are some ways to find a good mentor:

- Look for successful individuals in your industry and approach them to inquire if they offer mentorship.
- Ensure you treat them with respect and value their time.
- Maintain open communication and be honest.
- Remember, transparency is the cornerstone of building long-lasting relationships.

The Bottom Line

Building a strong network is an ongoing process that demands effort, dedication, and a genuine desire to connect with others. I've already shared some practical strategies to expand your professional circle. Ensure you implement these strategies and reap the benefits in the future.

***

Insights From Ifeoma Okwor

Dr. Ifeoma Okwor holds a Doctor of Veterinary Medicine (DVM) degree. She was trained in Nigeria and then moved to Canada, where she completed her Master's in Immunology and a Ph.D. in Medical

Microbiology. After that, she completed a three-year postdoctoral fellowship, focusing on asthma and septic shock. Currently, she serves as a program manager at Genome Prairie. Genome Prairie is a non-profit research funding and management organization serving the provinces of Saskatchewan and Manitoba. Genome Prairie is one of the six Genome Centers in Canada, which comprise the genomic enterprise along with Genome Canada.

Her role involves overseeing funded projects across various initiatives launched by Genome Canada.

What influenced your transition into the industry?

"Towards the end of my postdoc, I became pregnant and decided to stay home with my child for the first five years, but I couldn't wait that long. I needed mental stimulation beyond caring for my baby.

"During that time, I realized I missed being part of the scientific conversation, but didn't miss the lab work.

"I decided not to pursue a career in academia, but wanted to stay connected to the science ecosystem. I started looking into other opportunities and eventually transitioned into the Research Administration."

What skills do you find most transferable from academia to industry?

"Personality and interpersonal skills are crucial. In the industry, people must trust and feel comfortable working with you".

"Technical skills can be learned, but being a likable and reliable person makes a significant difference. It's essential to be someone who can be trusted to deliver on commitments and communicate effectively."

What advice would you give to graduate students or academics considering transitioning to a non-academic career?

"Be intentional about your career path. Identify where you want to go and what skills or certifications you need. Make a plan and start working towards acquiring those skills.

"**Networking** is crucial—talk to people, attend conferences, and seek out professional organizations relevant to your field. And remember, it's essential to think outside your research and be open to new opportunities and experiences."

CHAPTER 5: Job Search Strategies—From Application to Interview

When transitioning from academia to industry, it's crucial to make a strategic shift while searching for jobs in your field. The days of sending research-focused applications are over; it's time to demonstrate how your knowledge has been applied in the real world and how it aligns with your industry.

In this chapter, I'll share the relevant strategies for job applications, interview techniques, and ways to help you secure your dream position.

Targeting Right Fit

Aspiring professionals must be laser-focused on their area of interest to achieve success. However, transitioning to the industry requires a broader perspective. Conduct a proactive job search and identify companies that align with your goals.

Here are some strategies to conduct targeted research for the right job:

Research Your Industry

When you understand your industry, you are empowered to create a resume that perfectly aligns with its unique demands. Moreover, you actively seek out companies that are specifically looking for individuals with your academic background and skill set.

Networking

As mentioned in earlier chapters, networking is crucial for finding a suitable job and expanding your network of valuable connections. Similarly, it helps individuals find the ideal job. You can connect with alums working in your desired field and seek their assistance in identifying your perfect fit. Remember, even casual interactions with them can be beneficial. Therefore, maintain contact, attend conferences, meetings, and other events to enhance your chances of securing a rewarding job.

Customize Cover Letters and Job Applications

The following strategy is to personalize your cover letters and applications to increase your chances of securing the job. Here are some key elements that recruiters seek in your cover letters and applications:

- **Highlight relevant achievements:** When writing a cover letter or completing job applications, be sure to emphasize the achievements that are most closely aligned with the job requirements. Share details about your academic achievements, demonstrate your research skills, and mention your problem-solving capabilities. Ultimately, you want to ensure that you are translating your achievements into skills that are required for the job.

- **Mention transferable skills:** Discuss the transferable skills you possess and how you've excelled through experiences. Highlight your critical thinking abilities, adaptability, and communication skills, which are relevant to various industries.
- **Discuss relevant experience:** If you have experience that aligns with the job posting, be sure to mention it in both your cover letter and job application. Elaborate on your accomplishments during that experience. Doing so will enhance your profile's credibility and increase your chances of securing the job.

Interview Preparation

After successfully getting a response through your cover letter, it's time to ace the interview. However, let me clarify that interviews in an industry differ significantly from those in academia.

Here's how you can prepare for your job interview:

Prepare for Some Common Industry Questions

Before entering the interview room, it's essential to be prepared for some common questions that are often asked during interviews. I've listed a few of them below (but remember to conduct your research as well):

- Tell me about yourself.
- What are your career goals?
- Why are you interested in working with this company?
- Why would you want to work for this specific position?
- Tell me about your strengths and weaknesses

Note: *Don't share your weaknesses as they are, but frame them in a*

positive light.

- Do you have any questions for us?

Mock Interviews and Feedback

Since practice makes perfect, you can prepare for your real interview by conducting mock interviews with your friends. Ask them to interview you and provide feedback on your answers, as well as areas for improvement. This feedback can help you refine your communication style and body language. Additionally, you can seek insights from online friends in your aspiring industry.

Bridge the Gap Between Academia and Industry

During the interview, be sure to share your academic experiences that showcase the skills valued by the industry. For example, discuss research projects that demonstrate your ability to manage complex tasks, analyze data, and draw meaningful conclusions. By highlighting these experiences, you can increase your chances of becoming a desirable candidate and effectively demonstrate your management skills.

Post-Interview Success

Remember that the post-interview stage is crucial after you believe you've aced the job interview.

Here's what you should do afterward:

Follow Up

It is crucial to follow up within 24 to 48 hours of your interview. A well-crafted follow-up email can leave a lasting impression and demonstrate your enthusiasm for the position.

- **Begin with gratitude and appreciation:** Start your email by expressing your gratitude to the interviewer for the opportunity. A simple expression of gratitude can set a positive tone for the rest of your message.
- **Reiterate your interest:** Share why you are particularly interested in the position. Mention a specific point discussed during the interview that resonated with you. This demonstrates that you were attentive and engaged throughout the conversation.
- **Inquire about next steps:** Politely ask about the next steps in the hiring process. This demonstrates your eagerness to proceed and helps you stay informed about the timeline.

Example of a Follow-up Email

Subject: Thank You for the Interview Opportunity
Email:
Dear [Interviewer's Name],

Thank you for taking the time to interview me for the [Position] role at [Company Name]. I truly appreciate the opportunity to discuss how my skills and experiences align with your team's goals.

I am particularly excited about [specific points discussed during the interview], and my background in [relevant experience] will allow me to contribute effectively to [Company Name].

Could you kindly inform me about the next steps in the hiring process?

Thank you once again for considering my application.

Best regards,

[Your Name]

Offer Negotiation

If you receive a job offer, it's essential to negotiate favourable terms for yourself. Be clear about your expectations and maintain a professional tone. Here's how you can effectively negotiate:

- **Research is key:** Research the industry's standard salary package for the role. Utilize online data and seek advice from your network to get an idea of the salary range. This will help you determine whether to negotiate or not.
- **Confidence is necessary:** Now, it's time to negotiate. Don't hesitate, but exude confidence. Show enthusiasm and effectively showcase your skills and strengths during negotiations.
- **Negotiate beyond salary:** Negotiation isn't just about salary. It would be wise to discuss the benefits package, vacation time, flexible work arrangements, and other relevant details. Prioritize the offer that aligns with your priorities during the negotiation process.

Negotiation Script Sample

Here's how you can write a negotiation message/email after they send you an offer:

"Thank you for your offer. I'm pleased to work with you in [a specific role] and look forward to contributing value to your company. However, based on the market's salary trends, I was hoping for [a certain amount]. Nevertheless, I'm open to discussing other benefits of the job. Let's discuss."

Securing the Job

Congratulations! You've secured a job at your dream company. I understand the excitement, but remember, your success depends on your ability to thrive.

How will you ensure the quality of your work and maintain your job in the long run?

To help you achieve this, I'm creating a roadmap for the first few months. This roadmap will guide you in building trust with your employer and establishing yourself as a credible professional in the industry.

The Art of Onboarding

Onboarding is more than just signing a contract and taking office tours. It's an opportunity to create a positive first impression, gain a deep understanding of the company's culture and values, and establish yourself as a valuable teammate. Here are some tips to make the most of this period:

- **Be an active learner:** Don't just accept information; actively engage in the training process by asking thoughtful questions. Ensure that your doubts are cleared and seek additional resources when needed.
- **Be a culture chameleon:** When you join a new team, take the time to observe their culture. Understand their communication style, dress code, and other relevant aspects. Adapt to their culture

while preserving your unique identity and ensuring that it remains evident.
- **Network with others:** Introduce yourself to your team members and build connections. Attend company events, join lunch groups, and utilize internal social media groups to expand your network.
- **Use a proactive problem-solving approach:** Go beyond completing projects; actively identify potential roadblocks, propose solutions, and demonstrate initiative. By adopting this approach, you'll showcase your critical thinking and problem-solving skills.

Be Proactive in Communication

Building strong relationships requires effective communication skills and a willingness to share feedback. As an active team player, you can contribute in several ways:

- **Schedule regular check-ins**: Hold meetings with your manager to discuss your progress, clarify expectations, and address any concerns. This fosters a culture of open communication.
- **Offer constructive criticism:** Don't wait for feedback. As a team player, provide constructive feedback by suggesting improvements in processes, tools, or any areas you believe can be enhanced. By helping your colleagues succeed, you'll be valued.
- **Share your career goals:** Don't hide your career aspirations from your manager. Discuss your interests, growth opportunities, responsibilities, and plans. By sharing your goals, you'll become a source of motivation for your teammates.
- **Be a reliable source:** Become so valuable that your colleagues seek your advice. Actively listen to their questions, address their concerns, and volunteer to share your expertise whenever needed.

Learn Continuously

Your workplace is constantly evolving and progressing, so it's crucial to keep learning and growing. By continuously learning, you'll always stay ahead and become an A-player in your field. Here are some steps you can take to ensure constant learning:

- **Explore internal resources:** Start by utilizing the internal resources your company has made available. Take their courses, workshops, and mentorship opportunities to expand your knowledge and skills.
- **Embrace external learning:** Next, explore external resources to enhance your skills. Platforms like Coursera, Udemy, and others offer a wide range of courses in relevant areas. Additionally, attending industry events is an excellent way to stay current with the latest trends and best practices.
- **Develop soft skills:** As mentioned in previous chapters, soft skills are essential for versatility. Continuously learn new soft skills while you're working in the industry to enhance your profile further.
- **Share the knowledge you've learned:** Lastly, share what you've learned with others. It's said that knowledge increases when shared, and it's also a great way to retain what you've learned. Distribute your knowledge where needed to benefit others.

Maintain the Momentum

Remember, securing your dream job is a marathon, not a sprint. To win, you must maintain momentum throughout. Here are some tips to help you do that at your workplace:

- Keep taking on new challenges.

- Always maintain a positive attitude.
- Don't forget to maintain a work-life balance.
- Your personal life also matters.
- Lastly, keep learning while working on achieving your goals.

The Bottom Line

Congratulations on successfully transitioning from academia to industry! You've made significant strides from securing your dream job to navigating the job search process and finally obtaining employment.

However, remember that success is not a one-time achievement; it requires continuous effort, a willingness to learn, and a commitment to growth. To stay ahead, adopt a proactive approach and follow the strategies outlined in this chapter. By implementing these strategies, you'll be well on your way to securing good jobs at any stage of your career.

Success is a two-way street. When you put in the effort, your company thrives, and in return, you'll receive promotions and enhanced benefits. So, keep pushing forward and stay committed to your goals.

The greatest reward of all is the recognition and acknowledgment of your accomplishments, as well as the positive impact you make on the world. With that in mind, let's delve into the next chapter, where we'll explore even more valuable insights and strategies to enhance your career journey further.

* * *

Insights From Rachael Erdmann

Please briefly introduce yourself and describe your current role in government.
"My name is Rachael Erdmann, and I'm a senior policy advisor in the Department of Health for the Government of Alberta. I've been in this role for about 14 or 15 months. Before this, I spent five years as a research analyst with Alberta Health Services.

"My academic background includes a B.Sc. in Immunology and Infection from the University of Alberta and an MSc in Immunology from the University of Manitoba.

"After completing my MSc, I worked in a virology research lab in Edmonton while pursuing a Master of Public Health (MPH), focusing on health policy and management. This journey led me directly into Alberta Health Services and my current position.

"I wrote evidence synthesis reports for the Strategic Clinical Networks at Alberta Health Services. These networks connected operational leaders with research, clinicians, patients, and families, thereby driving innovation in Alberta. I also worked closely with the COVID-19 Scientific Advisory Group, first as a writer and later as a member of the Secretariat.

"My current role involves managing large-scale health evidence reviews in the Health Evidence and Policy Unit.

"We collaborate with health technology assessment teams within the University of Alberta, the Institute of Health Economics, and the University of Calgary to conduct these reviews."

What skills from your graduate studies were most transferable to your current role?
"Critical thinking, systems thinking, and writing skills were most transferable.

"My graduate studies taught me to analyze complex problems and understand their broader implications critically.

"Writing skills were crucial, particularly the ability to convey complex information to various audiences.

"Learning how to write succinctly for policymakers, who need actionable information rather than detailed methodologies, proved particularly important."

Were there any skills you had to improve when transitioning into government?

"I had to develop formal project management skills further. While I had some project management experience from academia, managing more extensive projects and coordinating diverse groups required additional skills. I also focused on improving my supervisory skills to manage and coordinate teams effectively."

What advice would you give to graduate students transitioning to non-academic roles?

"Articulate your transferable skills, such as collaboration, project management, time management, and writing. Don't limit yourself based on your academic background.

"Apply for roles that interest you, even if you don't meet every listed requirement.

"**Networking** is also crucial; while it can be challenging, especially for introverts, it opens many doors. For practical advice and resources, the "Ask A Manager" blog is invaluable for realistic job search and workplace guidance.

"Recognizing my transferable skills was crucial. For anyone transitioning into a new career, it's essential to remain open to opportunities based on what you think you're qualified for.

"This self-limitation tends to affect women more often than men. Job ads are essentially wish lists, not rigid requirements. Don't hesitate to apply if a role interests you and you believe you could excel in it.

"If you are applying for a job you aren't sure about, the worst response you can receive is a 'no,' and there's no shame. There's no risk if you adhere to professional norms. Following the application instructions provided by the company you're applying for is also crucial."

CHAPTER 6: Leveraging Academic Experience for Industry Success

We often wonder why we struggle to get hired or invited for an interview after submitting a robust CV and cover letter filled with years of experience, skills, and techniques.

I've pondered this too and faced similar challenges until I attended Dr. Ifeoma Okwor's workshop titled "Transferable Skills from Academic Research to a Non-Research Career."

During the seminar, Ifeoma, who has extensive experience as a hiring manager in the industry, discussed how she has encountered poorly written cover letters and resumes from experienced academics.

She noted that these candidates often list all the technical and scientific tasks they've completed in the lab and throughout their academic careers without tailoring their applications to the specific role or the role's requirements.

Consider This Scenario

Andrew walks into a bookstore and says, "I need a cookbook for a 5-year-old, specifically with baking content like cookies and muffins."

Sandra, the salesperson, responds, "Sure, I am a baker, a writer, and a cook; I've been doing this for five years."

What? Ridiculous right? This response, although informative, doesn't directly address Andrew's need. It doesn't confirm whether the book is available, nor does it demonstrate Sandra's effectiveness as a salesperson. Instead, it might lead Andrew to seek assistance elsewhere. This mirrors what often happens with job applications; while Sandra is undoubtedly skilled, her response must align with Andrew's request.

A more appropriate response would be, "Sure, I've been a cook, writer, and baker for five years, and this expertise helps me select the best children's cookbooks from our collection, including ones perfect for a 5-year-old interested in baking."

In this chapter, I will guide you through identifying, translating, and transferring your academic experiences to leverage industry success. I will start by crafting your CV and cover letter.

Identifying Your Skills

First, let's identify our skills and academic experiences. Understanding the specific technical skills you acquired through your educational background and how they can be applied in non-academic settings makes you versatile, enabling you to excel in diverse roles beyond academia.

Let's consider a few technical skills and explore how they translate into various soft skills.

- **PCR, ELISA, Flow Cytometry**

Soft Skills Derived: Technical proficiency, attention to detail, and the ability to handle complex procedures.

- **Data Analysis**

Soft Skills Derived: Analytical thinking, data-driven decision-making, and precision.

- **Laboratory Management and Inventory Control**

Soft Skills Derived: Organizational skills, efficiency, and reliability.

Reviewing Cover Letters and Resumes

Let's review samples of well-structured and poorly written cover letters and resumes based on job descriptions.
  Let's use this job description to create and review cover letters and resumes.

Industry Role: Research and Development (R&D) Scientist at BioDev Inventions Inc.
  Job Description:
  BioDev Inventions Inc. seeks a Research and Development Scientist to join our dynamic team. The ideal candidate will possess strong analytical skills, innovative thinking, a robust background in biological sciences, and excellent problem-solving abilities.
  Responsibilities include: Designing and conducting experiments, analyzing data, and collaborating with cross-functional teams. Contributing to the development of new products and technologies. The candidate should also demonstrate strong managerial skills and the ability to work effectively in a team.

Cover Letters—Poorly Written vs. Well-Written

CHAPTER 6: LEVERAGING ACADEMIC EXPERIENCE FOR INDUSTRY...

Cover Letter (Poorly Written)

Dear Hiring Manager,

I am applying for the Research and Development Scientist position. I hold a Ph.D. in Molecular Biology from XYZ University, where I conducted extensive research. I worked on genetic engineering and cellular biology projects and published some papers.

I used CRISPR-Cas9 and next-generation sequencing techniques. I also worked with other researchers. I am interested in working at BioDev Inventions Inc. I am eager to bring my expertise in molecular biology and my passion for translational research to your team.

Thank you for considering my application. I look forward to discussing how my skills and experiences align with BioDev Inventions' goals.

My resume is attached for your review.

Sincerely,

[Name]

Cover Letter (Well-Written)

Dear Hiring Manager,

I am excited to apply for the Research and Development Scientist position at BioDev Inventions Inc. With a Ph.D. in Molecular Biology from XYZ University and extensive research experience, I am confident that I can make a valuable contribution to your innovative team.

Below, I have highlighted how my background aligns with the requirements of this role:

Qualifications and Experience:

Strong Analytical Skills: In my doctoral research, I designed and conducted complex experiments, analyzed large datasets, and derived meaningful insights.

My proficiency in bioinformatics and data analysis, combined with my experience in genetic engineering and cellular biology, allows me to interpret complex biological data, solve problems, and present findings to diverse audiences.

Innovative Thinking and Contributing to New Products and Technologies: I have led research projects that have resulted in high-impact publications, demonstrating my ability to adapt and apply cutting-edge technologies, such as CRISPR-Cas9 gene editing and next-generation sequencing. My research has practical applications, contributing to the development of novel bioassays and experimental protocols. I am eager to bring my experience to BioDev Inventions Inc. to develop new products and technologies.

Robust Background in Biological Sciences: With a Ph.D. in Molecular Biology, I possess the technical knowledge and practical experience necessary for this role, covering genetic engineering, cellular biology, and bioinformatics.

Designing and Conducting Experiments: I independently designed and conducted experiments to ensure precision and reliability. I have also developed and optimized laboratory protocols, demonstrating my ability to manage and execute research projects effectively.

Collaborating with Cross-Functional Teams: Throughout my academic career, I have collaborated with interdisciplinary teams, refining my ability to communicate complex scientific concepts clearly and work effectively within diverse teams.

Problem-Solving Skills: Throughout my career, I have tackled challenging research questions and developed practical solutions, as evidenced by my successful projects and publications.

Managerial Skills: As a lab technician, I have experience managing lab operations and junior lab members to ensure efficiency and compliance with industry standards. I demonstrate organizational skills, efficiency, and reliability. BioDev Inventions' commitment to advancing healthcare through biotechnology aligns perfectly with my career goals.

I am eager to bring my expertise in molecular biology and my passion for translational research to your team.

Thank you for considering my application. I look forward to discussing how my skills and experiences align with BioDev Inventions' goals.

My resume is attached for your review.

Sincerely,

[Your Name]

PS: The cover letter samples focus on the body of the letter, while the resume samples focus on the work experience.

Resume - Poorly vs. Well-Written

Resume (Poorly Written)

Work Experience

Research Scientist/Lab Technician ABC Institution, [Year] - [Year]

- Conducted experiments using CRISPR-Cas9, PCR, ELISA, Flow Cytometry, and next-generation sequencing.
- Analyzed large datasets for product development. Worked with teams to develop bioassays and optimize protocols.
- Published research findings in journals.
- Solved research problems. Managed lab supplies.

Teaching Assistant XYZ University, [Year] - [Year]

- Helped teach molecular biology and genetics courses.
- Designed and graded lab assignments.
- Mentored students on research projects.
- Worked with faculty and students.

Resume (Well-Written)

Professional Experience

Research Scientist/Lab Technician ABC Institution, [Year] - [Year]

Pioneered experiments using advanced molecular biology techniques, including CRISPR-Cas9, PCR, ELISA, and flow cytometry: This experience aligns with the role's requirement to design and conduct experiments using advanced techniques, showcasing precision, attention to detail, and innovative thinking.

Analyzed large datasets to derive meaningful insights: Essential for the role's emphasis on data analysis to drive product development and innovation, demonstrating analytical thinking, critical interpretation, and data-driven decision-making.

Assisted senior scientists in the design and execution of experimental protocols: Demonstrated ability to work effectively with various departments, which is crucial for a collaborative R&D environment, highlighting teamwork, communication, and interdisciplinary collaboration.

Published research in high-impact journals: Highlights the ability to contribute to scientific advancements and effectively communicate findings, showcasing scientific writing and presentation skills and contributing to knowledge dissemination.

Solved complex research challenges: Showcases problem-solving skills and the ability to develop innovative solutions, crucial for R&D roles, demonstrating problem-solving, creativity, and resilience.

Managed lab inventories, ensuring the availability of essential reagents and equipment for ongoing projects.

This showcases my organizational and managerial skills, which are crucial for laboratory management.

It further highlights my ability to manage resources effectively and be a reliable team member.

Teaching Assistant XYZ University, [Year] - [Year]

Assisted in teaching molecular biology and genetics courses: Demonstrates foundational knowledge in biological sciences and the ability to communicate complex concepts, highlighting communication, instructional skills, and subject matter expertise.

Designed and graded laboratory assignments: Shows experience in creating and evaluating experiments, aligning with the need for experimental design in R&D, showcasing organizational skills, analytical thinking, and attention to detail.

Mentored students on research projects: Demonstrates leadership and the ability to guide and support research efforts, highlighting mentorship, leadership, and fostering a collaborative environment.

Promoted effective teamwork: It highlights the ability to work closely with others and enhance team dynamics, which is crucial for collaborative R&D settings. It showcases teamwork, collaboration, and interpersonal communication.

Comparison

What sets the well-written sample applications apart from the poorly written ones? Let's review!

Well-Structured Experience

- **Detail-Oriented:** Provides specific examples of responsibilities and achievements
- **Relevance:** Highlights how each task aligns with the job requirements for an R&D Scientist.
- **Impact:** Emphasizes contributions to new product development and lab improvements.
- **Skills Integration:** lists technical skills and demonstrates their application in work experience.

Poorly Structured Experience

- **Vague descriptions:** Uses generic terms without specific details or outcomes.
- **Lack of relevance:** The tasks are not connected to the R&D Scientist job requirements.
- **Minimal impact:** Fails to show the significance and contributions.
- **Skills listed separately:** Lists technical skills without showing their application to the role.

Length isn't a measure of quality in cover letters and resumes. It's not about how much you say but how clearly and effectively you connect your experiences and skills to the job role and its requirements.

When crafting these documents, focus on illustrating how your background makes you an ideal candidate by aligning your contributions and expertise with the position's needs.

This approach ensures that every word counts and directly supports your application.

Conclusion

By tailoring your job application to the specific role and its requirements, you can demonstrate to the employer that you understand their needs and are a suitable fit for the position.

I will conclude by giving you a brief task.

Regardless of your background or experience, prepare a cover letter and resume by tailoring your experiences to fit the job description below.

Job Description: Customer Service

Manager/Sales Representative Position Summary: This role combines customer service expertise with managerial skills. The ideal candidate must possess strong problem-solving, communication, and interpersonal skills. And be a team that manages and collaborates.

Key Responsibilities

Customer Service Management

- Oversee operations and resolve inquiries.
- Develop and implement service policies.
- Train and manage the team.
- Analyze service metrics.

Customer Service Representation

- Primary contact for key customers.
- Handle escalated issues.

- Provide product/service information.
- Relay customer feedback.

CHAPTER 7: Navigating the Corporate World—First 90 Days

Welcome to the corporate jungle! It's a vast ecosystem teeming with people, opportunities, competition, and, let's be honest, water cooler gossip. It's both exhilarating and intimidating for a relatively new professional like yourself.

You might be wondering, "How can I quickly win their hearts and become a leader in this fast-paced environment?"

Don't worry, intrepid explorer! I'm here to guide you through the blueprint to acing the first 90 days of your new industry journey.

I understand that you've transitioned from academia to the corporate world, and I've been there too. The initial transition can be daunting, but it's not as daunting as it seems. Our brains can sometimes make things seem more challenging than they are.

Fear not! I'll equip you with the tools and strategies you need to navigate the initial phase with ease and grace. So, let's dive into the details without further ado.

Marketer Scenario

Imagine yourself as a marketing associate joining a rapidly expanding company. Your primary responsibility is to help the company increase its awareness among millennials.

To facilitate a smooth transition and ensure a successful first 90 days, regardless of the industry, we will employ this persona.

Beginning the First 90 Days: Setting the Stage

The first 90 days carry significant value and weight in establishing yourself as a competent company employee. Thus, one must set realistic goals and expectations to navigate the transition smoothly by avoiding pitfalls.

Set Clear Objectives

After joining a company, the initial step is to set short-term goals for the first 30-60 days and long-term goals for 90 days and beyond. These goals should align with the following key points:

- **Company Expectations:** During the onboarding process, take the time to learn about the company's objectives and priorities. This knowledge will help you understand your role's responsibilities and how you can contribute to the company's success.

Revisiting Marketing Associate Scenario

As a marketing associate, you've learned that your company aims to boost brand awareness among millennials by up to 20% within a year. This aligns with their goal, and you'll set milestones or objectives to

CHAPTER 7: NAVIGATING THE CORPORATE WORLD—FIRST 90 DAYS

achieve it.

- **Your Aspirations:** After defining company goals, it's time to consider your aspirations. Do you aspire to become an expert social media marketer or a data scientist? Whatever your goals, remember to keep them in mind while setting clear objectives for the role.
- **Achievable Milestones:** Finally, it's time to set achievable milestones. Once you've listed your goals, considering the company's goals and objectives, break them into smaller milestones. Setting these milestones will help you track your progress and stay motivated. For instance, as a marketing associate, your first milestone could be attending a two-day workshop to enhance your skills in the first month.

Managing Expectations

Transitioning to a new role involves embracing the learning curve. Remember that challenges and adjustments are inevitable, but you must be prepared for them all to succeed.

For instance, if your company assigns you additional campaigns for their recently launched product, you should possess the skills to accept the challenge. You should be able to schedule, prioritize, and execute smooth operations despite the sudden change.

By managing these tasks with exceptional prowess while maintaining realistic expectations, you'll become the best team player in your first 90 days.

So, if an unexpected challenge arises, don't feel overwhelmed. Set achievable goals and work diligently towards them. You'll achieve your objectives.

Prioritizing Tasks

Prioritizing tasks also helps transition smoothly. Make sure you know how to prioritize tasks when assigned multiple tasks. You can begin by highlighting your key responsibilities and then work towards them individually.

Here's how you can prioritize tasks effectively:

- Grab a pen and paper.
- Write down all of your tasks on paper.
- Now, create categories. Put urgent tasks in the red category, moderate ones in the blue category, and those with extended deadlines and less importance in the green category.
- Begin working on them using the category to which they belong.

Taking Support

1. Leverage your network. Whenever you feel stuck, reach out to your seniors or other industry leaders for guidance and support to achieve your goals. Don't hesitate to seek help from your manager or HR if necessary. Remember, accepting support is a sign of strength, not weakness. You can also offer help and support to others in your network, as that's the essence of networking!

Key Takeaways

The key points to succeed in the transition from academia to industry in the first 90 days are:

- Set achievable goals.
- Manage expectations effectively.

CHAPTER 7: NAVIGATING THE CORPORATE WORLD—FIRST 90 DAYS

- Prioritize your tasks properly.
- Seek support where needed.

Remember, you have to align with the company's goals to succeed.

So, How Do You Align Your Work Style With the Company?

Aligning with your company's objectives provides you with a sense of direction and a solid purpose to keep moving forward. As a result, a mutually beneficial situation will arise. You'll gain growth opportunities and experiences while contributing to the company's success.

For instance, as a marketing associate, your primary responsibility will be to raise brand awareness and achieve the company's goals. Your personal goal is to become proficient in social media management tools. By working towards the company's objectives, you'll also be achieving your individual goals. This is how you can align yourself with corporate objectives.

Here are some ways to identify your work style and make informed decisions:

Self-Assessment: Evaluate your work style. Do you prefer open-minded explorations with flexible deadlines or clear goals with strict deadlines?

Communication Skills: Effective communication is crucial in the industry. You'll interact with team members, managers, and other stakeholders. Developing the ability to explain complex concepts in simple terms is essential, as not everyone will have the same level of technical understanding.

Project Management: Familiarize yourself with the basic principles of project management. This knowledge will help you manage your tasks and align with deadlines within the broader context of the industry.

Adaptability: Adaptability is vital to success in the industry. Be flexible enough to adapt to corporate culture and advancements, meeting market and customer expectations.

Unique and Valuable Team Player: Ensure you come across as a unique and invaluable team player. Let's help you achieve that as well.

How to Stand Out in the Corporate World?

Transitioning from academia to industry can be exhilarating, but it demands a significant mindset shift to navigate corporate expectations and stand out. The industry environment demands clear structures and expectations similar to those you encountered in academia. Here are some factors that can help you excel in your industry:

Networking: Connect with influential industry professionals to gain valuable insights and discover new opportunities.

Visibility: Showcase your accomplishments through publications, conferences, or industry-related blogs. Discussing your achievements strengthens your brand and positions you as an expert.

Skill Demonstration: Showcase your relevant industry skills through volunteer activities or work tasks.

Become a Subject Matter Expert: Utilize your academic knowledge and expertise to become your company's go-to person in that subject matter.

Seek Leadership Opportunities: Participate in activities that demonstrate your decision-making, team management, and leadership skills to contribute to your company's success.

Tips to Align Your Goals for Optimal Growth

Here are some tips to help you align your growth goals:

Identify transferable skills: Skills like communication, research, and critical thinking are easily transferable from academia to industry. Identify the skills you developed in academia and use them in the corporate world to align with its needs and achieve your goals.

Define your "win": Consider what a "win" looks like in your respective industry. Define your company's goals (both short-term and long-term) and work towards them.

Keep learning: Remember that the industrial world is ever-changing due to advancements and innovations. Being adaptable and continually learning new skills and techniques is crucial, as it enables you to adjust to changes and advance in your career.

Takeaways to Succeed in the Corporate World

Set clear expectations and goals.
    Track progress through KPIs.
    Focus on the results.
    Align your personal and professional goals.
    Practice open communication.
    Ask for feedback from your teammates or managers.
    Have a growth mindset.
    Build a good network.
    Be visible and demonstrate your skills in your industry.
    Be adaptable.

Adopting a Result-Driven Mindset to Thrive in Industry

The industry presents an opportunity for personal growth through a result-oriented mindset and practical application. To transition from academia to the industry, you must leverage and build upon the research and knowledge advancements. Adopting a result-oriented mindset is crucial in this process. Here's how you can achieve it:

- **Use a goal-driven approach:** When working in the industry, take a proactive approach to achieving goals and solving problems. Anticipate challenges and create solutions to stay ahead in your work setting. This will enhance your confidence and professional profile, helping you develop a result-driven mindset.
- **Measure the impact:** Since industry results measure success, ensure you monitor your performance and its impact on the real world. If the effect is positive, keep moving forward. If not, step back, analyze your strategies, and reapply your efforts.
- **Adopt a culture of accountability:** Take ownership of your work and ensure transparency in your communication. This approach builds trust with your teammates and keeps you committed to achieving your goals.

Adapting to a Goal-Oriented World to Master KPI Evaluations and Objectives

Since the industry thrives on KPIs and achieving goals, I'll guide you through setting and achieving goals in the corporate world to excel during your transition. Let's start with the basics!

Understanding the System:

- **Goal-oriented performance evaluations**: These evaluations analyze your performance based on predetermined goals, providing clear expectations and fair assessments. They also align with the company's objectives.
- **Key Performance Indicators (KPIs):** KPIs are measurable metrics that track progress toward set goals. Examples include sales figures, customer satisfaction scores, and project completion rates.

Adapting for Success:

- **Set goals:** To succeed in the industry, start setting goals, even if they seem simple, like getting a cup of coffee every morning for 30 days. Trust me, it's a roadmap to success.
- **Focus on outcomes:** Shift your mindset from task completion to outcome achievement. Put in efforts that generate results. Ask yourself, "Did my work help increase sales for the company?" and so on.

Strategies for Measurable Objectives:

- **Alignment is key:** Ensure that your objectives align with your personal goals and the goals of your dream company (conduct thorough research). This alignment will help both you and the company succeed together.
- **Break down goals:** Larger goals can be overwhelming. Break them down into smaller milestones and check them off your list as you accomplish each one. This approach will give you a sense of achievement and help you stay on track.
- **Track your progress:** While working on your personal or professional goals, monitor your progress towards key performance indicators (KPIs). This practice will help make necessary course

corrections and provide valuable data for future goal-setting processes.
- **Encourage open communication:** In a professional setting, maintain open communication with your team members, sharing your challenges, roadblocks, and successes.
- **Celebrate your achievements:** When you reach your set goals, take the time to celebrate them. This celebration will not only keep you motivated but also propel you towards further success.
- **Seek feedback:** While working in the industry, adopt a mindset of seeking feedback. Ask your manager or team members for their thoughts on your work. This way, you can identify errors and improve your work as it progresses.
- **Embrace a growth mindset:** Avoid adopting a fixed mindset in the industry. View challenges as opportunities and thrive through them. This approach will foster personal and professional growth, enabling you to adapt to industry changes effectively.

I trust you understand the goal-oriented nature of the industry and are prepared to adapt to its environment. By implementing the above strategies, you will gain an advantage in staying ahead and succeeding in any industry you may transition into.

The Bottom Line

The initial 90 days are pivotal in establishing your presence and making a name for yourself in the industry. To seize this opportunity, you must take immediate action and secure early victories. To ensure success during this crucial period, adhere to the strategies outlined in this chapter. Remember, these days are instrumental in laying the foundation for a promising career within the company. Go forth and make it happen!

CHAPTER 7: NAVIGATING THE CORPORATE WORLD—FIRST 90 DAYS

* * *

Insights From Reuben Saba and Ifeoma Okwor

I asked Reuben, **"What surprised you the most about working in the industry compared to academia?"**

He replied,

"The pace of the industry was a significant shift. Unlike academia, where projects can extend over years, the industry moves quickly, requiring adaptability and a broad understanding of science across multiple fields. This dynamic environment has broadened my scientific knowledge and continually engaged me."

I asked Ifeoma Okwor, **"Were there any challenges during your transition from academia to industry?"**

She replied,

"Absolutely. One significant challenge was adjusting to a different work environment and communicating effectively with a new audience. The flexibility I had in research was different from that in the industry, where interactions and meetings were more structured. Managing projects in unfamiliar fields, such as agriculture and the environment, also entailed a steep learning curve. The transition involved navigating new work cultures and adapting to different expectations and workflows."

CHAPTER 8: Overcoming Challenges: Common Hurdles and Solutions

The Titanic did not hit the iceberg because they did not see it coming, but because they could not change direction. –Dean Devlin

You're nervous about giving a presentation in your office for the first time. You're afraid of misstepping on a slide or getting lost in a maze of industry jargon. But fear not!

It's normal to feel nervous and make mistakes when trying something new. These experiences help us navigate the challenges and eventually reach our goals. I've been through this myself and can attest that the results have always been fruitful.

In this chapter, I'll help you overcome the challenges and hurdles that you might encounter during the first 90 days of your new role, often referred to as the transition phase.

Overcoming Imposter Syndrome in Your New Role

When transitioning, you might experience thoughts of inadequacy or ineligibility for tasks, which is impostor syndrome. You may question your abilities or qualifications, even feeling like a fraud in front of your colleagues. This is a familiar feeling, even among high achievers. Here are some strategies to help you deal with these feelings of doubt and impostor syndrome:

Acknowledge and Reframe

- **Recognize your feelings:** They are common and every academic experiences such feelings during transition.
- **Challenge your negative thoughts**: Replace phrases like "I don't belong here" or "I'm not good enough" with more positive affirmations, such as "This is just a new challenge" or "I will make it work."

Focus on Your Strengths

- **Make a list** of your achievements to boost your self-confidence and remind yourself of your capabilities.
- **Highlight Achievements:** When discussing with colleagues, look for opportunities to highlight past projects that had a positive impact.

Accept the Learning Curve

- **Embrace the support and ask questions** when needed. Remember, asking questions is not a sign of weakness.
- **Focus on your progress** and celebrate small wins and milestones as you acquire new industry knowledge and gain valuable experiences.

Remember, everyone makes mistakes, and it's okay not to be perfect. Learn from your mistakes and move on. Adjusting to a new environment takes time, but eventually, you'll become familiar with it. Be patient with yourself and embrace the learning process.

How to Build Self-Confidence

Building self-confidence is a gradual process that requires consistent effort and dedication. While it may not happen overnight, several strategies can be employed to achieve quick results.

Here are some valuable tips to boost your self-confidence:

- **Shift Your Perspective:** Challenge negative thoughts and replace them with positive affirmations. As mentioned earlier, this simple yet effective technique can make a significant difference in your self-perception.
- **Prioritize Self-Care:** When you take care of your physical and mental well-being, you naturally radiate confidence. Ensure you get enough sleep, eat a healthy diet, and engage in activities that nourish both your mind and body.
- **Embrace Continuous Learning:** Continuously seek new skills and expand your knowledge base. This not only enhances your abilities but also boosts your self-esteem and confidence.
- **Practice Confidence, Even When You Don't Feel It:** Sometimes, it's necessary to project confidence even when you're not entirely convinced of it. Stand tall, maintain eye contact, and speak in a clear voice. These actions can help you feel more confident and assertive.

Potential Challenges During Transition

Are you thrilled about landing your dream job? Before you get too excited, remember that every exciting career shift comes with its own set of challenges.

Here are some potential roadblocks you might encounter during your transition to a successful career in your desired industry:

Loss and Change

Loss and change are the first phase of transition. Leaving your comfort zone can be unsettling, and you may feel like you've lost your sense of identity. It's normal to experience sadness and a sense of loss during this phase.

Here are some tips to help you navigate this phase:

1. **Leaving the comfort zone:** Stepping outside your comfort zone can be challenging, and you might miss your role in academia.

- **Challenge:** "I miss the interaction and connection I had with my colleagues in my previous role. Overcoming social anxiety and building new connections is tough for me!"
- **Solution:** Get two coffees instead of one and offer them to start a conversation and overcome social anxiety.

2. **Grief and Identity:** Leaving a familiar place can be sad, and you might grieve a little and feel like you've lost your identity during the transition. This is another challenge that most people face.

- **Challenge:** Let's say you're moving from teaching to instructional design. That's a significant shift in your career. You might ask yourself, "Can I make an impact here?"
- **Solution:** Worry not. You simply need to utilize your transferable skills in situations like these. In this case, you can benefit from your communication and content engagement skills.

Emotional Challenges

Don't think that the transition doesn't affect you emotionally. It does, but you must know how to navigate these challenges. Remember, everything is normal, and you can find solutions.

Stress and anxiety: It can be stressful and lead to anxiety when you're introduced to new routines, expectations, goals, and people.

- **Challenge:** "Starting a new role has given me a lot of responsibility. My head aches."
- **Solution:** Take a deep breath and remind yourself that you're capable of handling the challenges ahead. Break down the tasks into smaller, manageable steps and focus on one step at a time. Practice mindfulness techniques and give yourself time to relax.

Feeling overwhelmed: It is common when you join a new position. You have a lot to learn, and it's easy to feel overwhelmed.

- **Challenge:** "It was so tough wrapping my head around that complex code."
- **Solution:** Ask your colleagues questions to gain a deeper understanding. Don't stress yourself or feel overwhelmed if something is out of your control.

Isolation and loneliness. It takes time to build connections with new people, especially if you were close to your previous team.

- **Challenge:** "Lunch breaks feel so lonely here."
- **Solution:** Introduce yourself to others and have lunch with them. Initiate making friends.

Practical Challenges

1. **Knowledge gaps:** Your new role may require you to learn new skills or acquire knowledge to adapt to the position, which can make you feel incompetent.

    - **Challenge:** "It's tough transitioning from a graphic designer to a UX designer."
    - **Solution:** Utilize online videos to enhance your learning. Don't let knowledge gaps hold you back.

2. **Performance expectations:** You might feel pressure to perform quickly and effectively, even while still learning, which can be challenging.

    - **Challenge**: "I might not analyze the data as well as expected by the team."
    - **Solution**: Communicate with your colleagues about the situation, take their cues, and do your best. Don't let impostor syndrome hinder your progress.

3. **Unexpected obstacles:** Unexpected challenges may arise, such as using new technology or facing unclear communication.

    - **Challenge:** For example, your company has launched two new products and wants you to design marketing campaigns quickly. You might wonder, "How do I handle this complex situation?"
    - **Solution:** Be adaptable, stay calm, prioritize tasks, and communicate clearly with your manager.

Climbing the Ladder: Challenges During Career Progression

As you contemplate leaving the familiar halls of academia for the dynamic corridors of the corporate world, you're undoubtedly envisioning an exciting leap forward. Yet, as you've discovered in this chapter, this transition has challenges. Every worthwhile endeavour comes with its own set of obstacles. Embracing this career progression means preparing to tackle these hurdles, but with determination, you can climb the ladder to success.

The industry requires skill sets, a quicker pace, and a results-oriented mindset. Although you may possess all or a few of these skills in your arsenal, and your academic background may provide a strong foundation, you will still face challenges and roadblocks while advancing in your career or transitioning.

However, don't worry. We have already made great strides in understanding how to navigate the transition and succeed in your career.

Here are some tips to help you climb the ladder while facing the challenges during career progression:

- **Adopt the "do" mentality.** While academia makes you a pro in theoretical research, the industry requires you to get it all done practically. So, adopt a solution-oriented approach and try doing things you can't do. Who knows, it might work.
- **Develop commercial intelligence.** It's your time to understand the business side of your company. Consider how your work benefits the company, and then tailor your approach accordingly. Remember, you are here to add value to your company so it can

succeed.
- **Become metrics-driven.** While publications used to be your academic benchmark, it's time to use metrics such as KPIs to stay ahead in the industry. Ensure you adapt to new success standards and continue to progress in your career.

Maintaining Motivation and Resilience

The truth is that setbacks are inevitable, whether in academia or industry. The real success lies in staying motivated and being resilient when adversity strikes.

How to Maintain Motivation

The following are some tips to stay motivated:

- Set clear goals with smaller milestones. Take your time setting bigger milestones.
- Refrain from dwelling on what-ifs. Keep moving forward by putting in your sincere efforts.
- Develop a growth mindset and believe you can overcome the challenges.
- Maintain a healthy routine. Don't overstress.
- Reconnect with your core values and aspirations to keep your passion alive and your career moving forward.

How to Stay Resilient

Here's how you can be resilient when facing adversities:

- Failures are your most significant friends. Learn from them and

move on.
- Self-reflect and develop perseverance to overcome the hurdles.
- Take support where needed. Refrain from a do-it-all-yourself attitude. You can always ask for help from your colleagues.

The Bottom Line

The initial days in the corporate world can be challenging, but they also offer numerous opportunities for learning, growth, and success. Embrace these challenges as opportunities for growth, seek support when needed, and celebrate your achievements. With a growth mindset and a willingness to learn, you'll eventually excel in your career.

Remember, transitioning is about learning and growing, so embrace this phase with open arms.

* * *

Insights From Ifeoma Okwor and Samuel Ogunsola

I asked Ifeoma Okwor, "Did you face any rejections while trying to secure a job during your transition?"

"Yes, I applied for a science policy position through MITACS but didn't get it. It was a position aimed at bridging the gap between science and policy, working with the Canadian Science Policy Centre. However, since moving to Canada, I've primarily worked in research roles, and the Statistics Canada job was my first experience outside of academia before landing my current role at Genome Prairie."

I asked Samuel Ogunsola, "What challenges do you anticipate in transitioning, and how do you plan to address them?"

"After the flexibility of academia, adapting to the structured environment of the workplace will be challenging. Moreover, securing optimal opportunities may take time. Adaptability and commitment to continuous learning and development will be crucial in overcoming these challenges."

CONCLUSION

I hope this book has been your steadfast companion throughout this transformative journey, guiding you from the realm of academic research to the industrial landscape.

I've covered everything from understanding the fundamental concepts to implementing practical strategies to streamline the process for you. I genuinely hope you've found it enjoyable and enriching.

Here are some key points to keep in mind during your transition:

- **Bridge the Gap:** Identify any knowledge or skill gaps and leverage your experiences to bridge them. Continuously acquire new skills and apply them in the industrial environment.
- **Build Your Brand:** As discussed in one of the chapters, creating a personal brand is vital for attracting the right opportunities. Dedicate time and effort to developing your brand.
- **Secure Your Dream Job:** Remember, landing the job requires the necessary skills. I hope you've gained valuable insights into job security.
- **Conquer Challenges:** I've already provided guidance on how to tackle hurdles and challenges. Ensure you apply the strategies in this book to overcome obstacles and emerge victorious in your industry. Challenges are growth opportunities.
- **Utilize Your Strengths:** Ultimately, it's time to leverage your strengths and contribute to your company by delivering valuable services and establishing yourself as an industry leader.

CONCLUSION

Your Action Plan for Success

Finally, it's time to embark on your journey. Here's a roadmap to guide you to success:

1. **Revisit** each chapter's strategies and align them with your goals.
2. **Write down** the specific actions you need to take to achieve your personal and professional objectives.
3. **Engage** with the community, including professionals, seniors, colleagues, alums, and more. Remember, seeking help is a sign of strength, not weakness.

Remember!
Beyond the Books" isn't just a book; it's a comprehensive guide that serves as a stepping stone to embarking on your career journey. Remember, this is merely the initial phase of building a successful career in the industry. Just as many accomplished academics have achieved their success, you too can do it efficiently.

The key lies in cultivating self-belief and persevering through the process. Ultimately, your willpower and commitment to your growth are the driving forces behind your success.

While transitioning may pose challenges at times, your unwavering determination to achieve greater heights will propel you forward. So, maintain your momentum and seize the opportunity to excel!
As Winston Churchill says,
"Success is Not Final, Failure is Not Fatal: it is the Courage to Continue that counts."

Answer It!

Lastly, do you remember the question I asked you in the introduction (page 5)?

I hope you can answer it now...

_____
_____
_____
_____
_____
_____
_____
_____
_____
_____
_____
_____
_____
_____
_____

REFERENCES

Churchill, W. (2019, February 20). Winston Churchill quotes. Forbes. https://www.forbes.com/sites/alejandrocremades/2019/02/20/15-powerful-quotes-on-success/

Devlin, D. (2024, April 9). Dean Devlin quotes. Indeed. https://www.indeed.com/career-advice/career-development/motivational-office-quotes

Gale, P. (2019, June 25). Porter Gale quotes. Hubspot. https://blog.hubspot.com/marketing/networking-quotes

Hyatt, M. (n.d). Michael Hyatt quotes. Jerome Joseph. https://jeromejoseph.com/personal-branding-quotes-captions/

Kaiser, R. B. R., Sherman, R. A., Hogan. R. (2023, March 07). *It takes versatility to lead in a volatile world.* Harvard Business Review. https://hbr.org/2023/03/it-takes-versatility-to-lead-in-a-volatile-world

Oxlade-Chamberlain, A. (n.d). Alex Oxlade-Chamberlain quotes. Brainy Quote. https://www.brainyquote.com/quotes/alex_oxladechamberlain_982152?src=t_versatility

Preparing students for their futures: The role of higher education. (2023, August 21). Quad C. https://www.quadc.io/blog/preparing-students-for-their-futures-the-role-of-higher-education

About the Author

Mary Chinyere Obiechina Ifeakandu is a passionate educator, neuroscientist-in-training, and advocate for career development and youth empowerment. She is currently pursuing a PhD in Physiology at the University of Manitoba, Canada, with a research focus on spinal cord sensory-motor integration. Mary began her academic career as a university lecturer in Nigeria, where she taught and mentored undergraduate students in the medical sciences.

Her journey spans diverse professional environments, including business, entrepreneurship, managerial roles, and customer relations, where she has honed a unique blend of leadership, adaptability, and problem-solving skills. These skills complement her academic pursuits and have enriched her approach to mentorship, project execution, and community impact.

Beyond the classroom, Mary has led several initiatives across Canada and Nigeria, championing mentorship, community service, and science advocacy, particularly among young women in STEM. She is the founder of multiple outreach programs supporting student transitions, vocational training, and leadership development.

Beyond the Books is a reflection of her own dynamic experiences and those of others who have successfully navigated career transitions. With this book, she continues her mission to bridge the gap between education and the evolving demands of the professional world.

www.ingramcontent.com/pod-product-compliance
Lightning Source LLC
Chambersburg PA
CBHW050329010526
44119CB00050B/731